1 MONTH OF
FREE
READING

at

www.ForgottenBooks.com

By purchasing this book you are eligible for one month membership to ForgottenBooks.com, giving you unlimited access to our entire collection of over 1,000,000 titles via our web site and mobile apps.

To claim your free month visit:
www.forgottenbooks.com/free896870

ISBN 978-0-266-83731-2
PIBN 10896870

NEW YORK

HENRY HOLT AND COMPANY

1905

YALE STUDIES IN ENGLISH

ALBERT S. COOK, Editor

XXIV

AN INDEX TO
THE OLD ENGLISH GLOSSES
OF THE DURHAM HYMNARIUM

BY

HARVEY W. CHAPMAN

NEW YORK

HENRY HOLT AND COMPANY

1905

OXFORD: HORACE HART
PRINTER TO THE UNIVERSITY

PREFACE

THE following Index was compiled [1] in 1896 from an Old English Hymnarium, edited for the Surtees Society in 1851 (Vol. 23) by Stevenson, under the title, *The Latin Hymns of the Anglo-Saxon Church, with an Interlinear Anglo-Saxon Gloss ; derived chiefly from a Manuscript of the Eleventh Century preserved in the Library of the Dean and Chapter of Durham.* The Latin text of this manuscript was collated with that of MSS. Cott. Jul. A. VI, and Cott. Vesp. D. XII.

Of the dialect Stevenson remarks : 'The interlinear gloss is an indisputable specimen of Western Saxon. Its age is probably a little later than the Norman Conquest.' Notwithstanding this confident assertion, it will be seen that the language shows clear traces of Kentish influence.

In a footnote to p. viii, Stevenson says : 'If the Editor might venture to hazard a conjecture, founded on nothing more definite than the style of writing and the general appearance and execution of the book, he would be inclined to attribute its origin to Winchester. According to Rud (*Catalog. MSS. Codd. Ecclesiae Dunelm.*, p. 174), it was given to the

---

[1] In candidacy for a senior prize offered by Professor Cook.

Library of Durham by Thomas Wharton, Esq.'
The assignment of its origin to Winchester is of
course rendered very doubtful by the frequent
occurrence of Kentish forms.

According to Stevenson, two scribes were engaged
in the work of glossing, the second belonging to
a somewhat later period than the first; however,
this difference of hands seems to have little practical
importance as respects our immediate purpose.

The peculiarities of the Latin spelling of the
period have been reduced to the more usual forms.
As to the forms of the Old English head-words of
the Index, the attempt has been made, in cases
where there is a variation of the stem-vowel—as,
for example, between WS. *y* and Kent. *e*—to employ
for the head-word the vowel which preponderates,
and introduce cross-references from the less common
forms to this.   Where þ occurs, its place has always
been taken by ð.   A superior category, followed by
inferior ones, is entered only once under each head-
word; for instance, 'ind.' is not repeated under a
verb, when various tenses of the indicative occur.
Where no Old English form is quoted, it is to be
understood that the form is in all respects identical
with the head-word.   There are a few manifest
errors in the text as printed; these have been
reproduced as they occur.

The Latin-Old English Index will, it is hoped, be
useful to scholars in various ways.

A

ābūgan sv. *cedere*, opt. pres. 3 pl. abugan 14.18; 99.7.

ac conj. *sed*, 11.7; 36.15; 37.16; 43.18; 61.18; 62.11; 97.11; 103. 6; 115.5; 130.13; 132.15.

ācænnan wv. *edere, eniti, generare, gignere, nasci, parturire, parere,* ind. pres. 2 sg. acenst 110.8; pret. 2 sg. acendest 109.6; 3 sg. acende 47.6; 50.17; acænde 54. 10; 139.2; acænede 140.3; ger. to acennenne 103.1; pres. p. nsm.acænnende 39.12; 53.4; pp. acenned 111.9; acænned 40.9; 141.10; nsm.acenned 45.9; 77.5; 104.5; acænned 36.3; 43.1; 103. 6; 108.8; dsmn. acænnedum 47. 15; 139.17; asm. acennedne 31. 17; acænnedne 42.9; 42.15; 47. 6; 48.5; 109.5; vsm. acænned 39.4; 141.2.

ācōligan wv. *tepescere*, opt. pres. 3 sg. acolige 26.16.

ādīlegian wv. *delere*, ind. pres. 3 pl. adilegiað 141.14; pret. 3 sg. adyligode 6.16; 3 pl. adilogodon 128.7; opt. pres. 2 sg. adilegie 5. 10; 3 sg. adilegie 20.5; imp. sg. adilega 133.12.

ādl sf. *languor, morbus*, ns. adl 122.14; ds. adle 137.7; as. adle 8.15.

ādlig adj. *aeger, aegrotus, languens, languidus, morbidus*, asm.

adligne 34.12; asf. adlige 29.11; 127.4; npm. adlige 19.2; gpm. adligra 137.6; dpm. adligum 7. 4; 62.13; apm. adlige 116.15.

ādrǣfan wv. *depellere, expellere, pellere, repellere*, ind. pret. 3 sg. adræfde 64.8; opt. pres. 2 sg. adræfe 91.19; 92.17; 115.9; 3 sg. adræfe 8.15; 27.16; 37.3; 113.13; 116.10; 127.11; imp. sg. adræf 18.7; 23.17; 28.13; 77.1; 104.17; pl. adræfað 119. 8; inf. adræfan 32.18; pres. p. nsm. adræfende 74.2; pp. adræfed 142.4.

ādrēogan sv. *ducere*, inf. adreogan 8.4.

ādrēogenlic adj. *gerens*, gsn. adreogenlices 103.2.

ādrīgan wv. *abstergere, tergere*, opt. pres. 3 sg. adrige 26.11; imp. sg. adrig 128.8; adryg 23. 2; inf. adrigan 49.2.

ādwǣscan wv. *extinguere*, imp. sg. adwæsc 10.14.

ǣ sf. *lex*, gs. ǣ 66.2; 94.12.

ǣdbrēdan, see ǣtbrēdan.

ǣddre sf. *fibra*, dp. æddrum 102.1.

ǣfen sm. *vesper*, gs. æfenes 13. 16; ds. æfene 34.14; 61.11; as. æfen 11.5; 24.18; 82.9.

æfengereordung sf. *cena*, ds. æfengereordunga 82.1.

æfenglōmung sf. *crepusculum*, as. æfenglommunge 16.16.

æfestig adj. *invidus*, gsm. æfestigan 16.2.

æfre adv. *semper, umquam*, æfre 12.18; 30.16; 32.17; 32.19; 32.22; 60.11; 72.17; 76.12; 77.10; 88.12; 109.10; 117.2; 119.3; 129.7; 139.18; 145.4; 146.16.

æfter prep. with dat. *post*, 54.11; 82.3; 89.11; 106.10; 140.11.

æfterfyligan wv. *sequi*, pres. p. gpf. æfterfyligendra 14.16.

æfterfyligendnyss sf. *successus*, dp. æfterfyligendnyssum (?).

æghwær adv. *ubique*, æghwær 42.7.

æghwæðer pron. *uterque*, nsm. æghwæðer 103.10; gsm. æghwæðeres 93.5; 139.18.

æghwanone adv. *undique*, æghwanone 46.6.

ælc adj. pron. *omnis*, nsnf. ælc 5.4; 6.11; 30.4; 31.18; 108.10; 142.4; gsn. ælces 108.13; dsmn. ælcum 83.9; 136.15; dsm. ælcan 27.17; dsf. ælcere 73.13; 86.18; 93.6; 97.1; 121.6; 139.19; asm. ælcne 53.15; asn. ælc 14.7; 37.8; 93.2; 115.11; asf. ælce 8.14; 141.20; ælc 137.12.

ælmihtig adj. *cunctipotens, omnipolens, tonans*, gsm. ælmihtigan 27.5; asm. ælmightigan 8.13; vsm. ælmihtiga 12.1; 57.15; almihtig 146.4.

ænde sm. *finis*, ds. ænde 47.16; 83.19; 123.4; 145.5; ændan 27.17; as. ende 33.16.

ændebyrdnyss sf. *ordo, series*, ds. endebyrdnysse 28.11; 38.1; as. ændeberdnyssa 22.13; endebyrdnysse 103.2; ds. (?) endebyrdnys 103.3.

ængel sm. *angelus*, ns. ængel 72.18; 75.8; 85.10; 85.15; 116.9; gs. ængles 91.5; ds. ængle 82.10; as. ængel 116.5; 116.13; np. ænglas 42.14; 87.9; englas 51.8; gp. ængla 108.6; 114.17; 116.1; 117.1; 145.16; 147.3; dp. ænglum 113.5; 136.3; 138.9; ap. ænglas 60.10.

ængelic adj. *angelicus*, npn. ængellice 118.1; dpn. engelicum 111.21.

ænglisc adj. (*Angli*), *Anglicus*, gsf. ængliscre 98.5; gpm. ængliscra 99.4; 129.6.

ænig pron. *quisquam*, nsm. ænig 104.5.

ænlic adj. *aureus*, nsn. ænlic 24.3; dsn. ænlicum 105.10; vsmn. ænlic 127.1.

æppel sm. *pomus*, as. æppel 31.7.

ær adv. *ante*, ær 31.14; 74.9.

ær prep. *ante*, ær with dat. 11.10; 30.15; 39.3; with acc. (Latin construction) 34.3; 59.15; 115.20; 125.10.

ærest adv. *primum*, 7.13; 14.14; 28.1.

ærmergen sm. *mane*, ns. ærmergen 30.9.

ærnemergen ѕm. *mane, diluculum*, ns. ærnemergen 16.14; as. ærnemergen 13.16.

æswicung sf. *scandalum*, as. æswicunga 80.15.

æt prep. with acc. *ad*, 136.5.

ætbēon anv. *adesse*, ind. pres. 2 sg. ætbist 36.9; pret. 3 sg. ætwæs 49.5; opt. pres. 3 sg. ætsy 99.11; imp. sg. ætbeo 13.10; 64.9; 64.10; 147.2; inf. ætbeon 14.13.

ætbrēdan sv. *auferre, ferre, tollere, rapere, subtrahere*, ind. pret. 3 sg. ætbræd 52.10; ædbræd 76.1; æbbræd 79.6; opt. pres. 2 sg. ætbrede 133.4; pret. 2 sg. ætbrude 84.4; pp. apm. ædbrodene 49.13.

ætforan prep. with dat. *coram*, 124.15.

æðelborenyss sf. *stemma*, gs. æðelborenysse 47.7.

æðele adj. *egregius, inclitus, gloriosus, nobilis*, gsm. æðelys 38.6; dsm. æðelum 84.7; 87.12; 105.12; dsmnf. æðelan 46.18; 73.17; 85.5; asm. æðelne 79.10; asnf. æðele 54.1; 124.17; vsmf. æðele 79.16; 106.3; 110.5; 125.11; 128.1; 131.5; apm. æðela 132.1; vpm. æðelan 119.13.

æthrīnan sv. *attingere*, ind. pret. 3 sg. æðran 52.8.

æðrȳtness, see āðrētnyss.

æt nēxtan adv. *demum, tandem*, æt nextan 36.8; 36.13.

ætslīdan sv. *labi*, pp. apm. ætslidan 7.7.

ætspurnan sv. *offendere*, inf. 67.6.

ætspyrning sf. *offensum*, dp. ætspyrningum 142.3.

ætstandan sv. *assistere, retundere*, ind. pres. 2 sg. ætstandest 33.14; opt. pres. 3 sg. ætstente 16.2; ætstentan 70.10.

ætwunigan wv. *assistere, astare*, ind. pres. 3 sg. ætwunað 42.15; opt. pres. 3 sg. ætwunige 117.2; imp. sg. ætwuna 18.4.

ætȳwan wv. *ostendere*, imp. sg. ætyw 43.14; pp. npf. ætiwde 86.11.

āfandigan wv. *probare*, ind. pret. 2 sg. afandode 72.16.

āfeormigan wv. *abluere, expiare, purgare*, ind. pres. 3 sg. afeormað 91.7; opt. pres. 2 sg. afeormige 23.10; 133.4; 1 pl. afeormian 14.8; 3 pl. afeormian 118.12; imp. sg. afeorma 53.15; pres. p. nsm. afeormigende 52.10; pp. npm. afeormode 22.4; 65.7; apm. afeormode 46.13; afeormodan 4.11; apn. afeormoda 27.18.

āfestnigan wv. *configere*, pp. nmp. afestnode 78.5.

āflȳgan wv. *arcere, fugare*, opt. pres. 2 sg. aflyge 71.2; imp. sg. aflyg 18.6; pres. p. nsm. afligende 133.13; pp. npm. afligede 23.12.

āforhtigan wv. *pavescere*, pres. p. nsf. aforhtigende 139.10.

áfyrsigan wv. *auferre*, opt. pres. 2 sg. afyrsige 23.9; 3 sg. afyrsige 114.7; imp. sg. afyrsa 10. 15; pl. afyrsiað 19.1; afersiað 120.3; pres. p. nsm. afyrsigende 104.2.

ágéangesǽndan wv. *refundere*, pp. ageangesǽnd 136.11.

ágeldan, see ágyldan.

ágen adj. *proprius*, dsn. agenū 125.5; asm. agenne 108.14.

ágéotan sv. *effundere, fundere, profundere, refundere*, pres. ind. 1 pl. ageotað 98.14; inf. ageotan 52.17; pres. p. nsm. ageotende 42.17; 79.7; 134.11; pp. agotan 130.12; dsn. agotenum 139.11; dpm. agotenum 65.2.

ágyfan sv. *reddere*, ind. pret. 3 sg. agæf 79.14; opt. pres. 2 sg. agyfe 91.20; pret. 2 sg. ageafe 64.5; 3 sg. ageafe 20.2; imp. agyf 115.13; pres. p. nsm. agyfende 140.8; npm. agyfende 123.2; pp. agyfan 83.2.

ágyldan sv. *reddere, rependere*, ind. pres. 2 sg. agyldst 47.13; 76.2; 3 sg. ageldað 4.12; opt. pres. 3 sg. agylde 27.10; 1 pl. agyldan 86.18; pres. p. nsm. agyldende 36.11; npm. ageldende 57.12; pp. agolden 136.10.

ágyltan wv. *delinquere*, ind. pret. 1 pl. agiltan 26.10; agyltan 124.15; 131.12.

áhębban sv. *levare, tollere*, ind. pres. 1 pl. ahebbað 21.1; opt. pres. 3 sg. abebbe 25.14.

áhnigan wv. *possidere*, ind. pres. 3 pl. ahniað 105.17.

áhōn rv. *suspendere*, pp. ahangen 78.4.

áidlian wv. *evacuare, vacare*, inf. aidlian 47.12; pp. aidlod 125. 14.

álýsan wv. *liberare, redimere, solvere*, ind. pret. 2 sg. alysdest 31.13; 125.5; opt. pret. 3 sg. alysde 4.4; imp. sg. alys 20.14; 42.6; pres. p. nsm. alysende 50.7; 53.7; 84.6; pp. nsn. alysed 83.1; npmf. alysede 40.5; 76.8; dpm. alysedum 32.20; 80.12; 105.4; 117.14.

álýsednyss sf. *redemptio*, gs. alysednysse 78.7; ds. alysednysse 59.10; vs. alysednyss 83.16.

Álýsend sm. *Redemptor*, nvs. alysend 5.9; 23.16; 26.17; 34. 8; 39.1; 41.1; 43.13; 48.2; 53. 9; 79.16; 90.9; 104.20; 112. 10; 117.13; 117.20; 119.1; 124.5; 124.17; 131.1; 137.17.

ámearcigan wv. *annotare*, pp. apm. amearcode 73.9.

ámýtan wv. *pinguere*, ind. pres. 2 sg. amytst 22.9.

án adj. *solus, unus*, nvs. an 10.2; 29.5; 34.2; 55.7; 59.14; 65.14; 68.11; 73.13; 77.18; 105.8; 115.19; 121.6; 137.16; 139.19; nvs. ana 28.6; 33.12; 39.3; 39.15; 140.3; gsf. anre 42.3; dsmn. anum 1.11; 25.7; dsf. anre 115. 14; 120.17; 145.7; asm. ænne 3.15; 21.17; 146.17.

án adv. *tantum*, 103.20.

anbídigan wv. *expectare, praestolari*, ind. pres. 1 pl. anbidiað 5. 15; 30.10; inf. anbidian 90.4.

áncænned ptc. *natus, unicus, unigenitus,* nvs. ancænned 53.
1; 67.2; 79.15; 99.8; 99.9; 99.
10; nsn. ancenned 73.12; gsf.
ancænnedre 106.7; dsm. ancen-
nedū 45.18; ancænnedan 120.
8; asm. ancænnedne 50.4; an-
cennedne 133.7; vsm. ancæn-
neda 5.18; 27.5; 39.2; ancen-
nede 72.6.

ancsum adj. *anxius,* apf. anc-
sume 2.8.

and conj. *atque, -que,* 7.17; 21.
4. Elsewhere 7 = *et.*

andetnyss sf. *confessio,* ns. 118.
10; as. andetnysse 10.6.

andettære sm. *confessor,* ns. andettære 136.17; 138.4; dp. an-
dettærum 131.14; vp. andette-
ras 119.14.

andettan wv. *confiteri, fateri,*
ind. pres. 1 pl. andettað 43.2;
3 pl. andyttað 35.4; andettað
86.14; opt. pres. 3. pl. 48.11; 52.
2; ger. to andettenne 20.17; pres.
p. npm. andettende 23.7; gpm.
andettendra 131.6; dpm. andet-
tendum 33.6; 62.11.

andfænge adj. *acceptabilis,* npn.
andfænge 63.6.

andget sn. *sensus,* ns. 10.5; ds.
andgite 3.9; dp. andgitum 7.
11; 27.15; 28.2; andgytum 15.
15.

andweard adj. *praesens,* nsm.
andweard 39.13; nsn. andwerd
137.3; apn. andwyrde 119.7.

andweardigan wv. *praesentare,*
pres. p. nsm. andweardiende
89.7.

andwlita wm. *vultus,* gs. andwlitan 124.18; ds. andwlitan 21.
16; 22.6; 94.14; anwlitan 84.12;
143.2 ; as. andwlitan 31.4 ; dp.
andwlitum 89.7.

ánfeald adj. *simplex, singularis,*
dsn. anfealdum 21.18; vsm. an-
feald 105.2; vsnf. anfealde 63.
5; 77.11.

anginn sn. *cardo, exordium,
initium, principium, primordium,*
ns. anginn 14.17; ds. anginne
39.3; 50.1; as. anginn 109.7;
109.8; dp. anginnum 22.17.

ánlīe adj. *unicus,* dsm. anlicū
45.5.

anlīcnyss sf. *imago,* gs. anlic-
nysse 31.3.

ánnyss sf. *unitas,* ds. annysse
106.13; vs. annyss 1.3; 63.5;
146.9; annys 26.1; 145.14;
147.1.

ansīen sf. *facies,* as. ansine 86.
5; anseon 97.17.

anðrācigan wv. *inhorrere,* ind.
pret. 3 sg. anðracode 132.5.

anweald smn. *imperium, potestas,* ds. anwealde 82.12; 106.
1; 124.11.

anwlita, see andwlita.

apostol sm. *apostolus,* nvs. apostol 38.5; 129.6; nvp. apostolas
85.11; 86.4; 87.5; 119.10; gp.
apostola 122.3; 123.9; dp. apo-
stolum 61.6; 85.20; 96.7; 113.
6; 118.7.

árǣcan wv. *porrigere,* opt. pres.
3 sg. aræce 4.10.

ārǣran wv. *suscitare*, opt. pres. 3 sg. arære 3.12.

ārǣrend sm. *excitator*, ns. 18.15.

ārfæst adj. *pius*, nvs. arfæst 37.16; 48.2; 104.20; 126.10; 137.1; 145.10; arfæsta 97.16; 98.15; 117.15; 126.1; dsm. arfæstan 8.1; asm. arfæste 53.16; arfæstan 4.7; dpmf. arfæstum 57.1; 137.11; apn. arfæste 127.10; sup. vsm. arfæstesta 5.17; 10.9; 10.18; 11.9; 15.17; 17.9; 17.17; 94.13; 115.10; 134.14; 138.15; arfæsteste 14.9.

ārfæstlīce adv. *pie*, 121.4.

ārfæstnyss sf. *pietas*, ns. arfæstnyss 84.9; 135.18; gs. arfæstnysse 106.7; ds. arfæstnysse 8.16; arfæstnyssa 120.17.

ārigan wv. *parcere*, imp. sg. ara 105.4; 139.14; 62.11; pres. p. nsm. arigende 84.11; 131.14.

ārīsan sv. *consurgere, exsurgere, resurgere, surgere*, ind. pres. 3 sg. arisð 24.3; 83.3; 1 pl. arisað 14.11; 20.17; pret. 2 sg. arise 83.12; 3 sg. aras 85.6; 85.9; opt. pres. 3 sg. arise 27.8; arisa 37.5; pres. p. arisende 4.3; 7.15; 40.12; dpm. arisendum 27.7; inf. arisan 4.6; 31.19; 86.13; arysan 6.17.

ārlēas adj. *impius*, nsn. arleasa 23.13; vsm. arlease 51.13; npm. arleasan 85.14.

ārwurðe adj. *honestus, venerandus*, nvs. arwurðe 54.5; 144.1; 145.11; sup. nsm. arwurðosta 34.16.

ārwurðigan wv. *venerare*, pres. p. nsm. arwurðiende 108.9; npm. arwurðigende 115.3.

āsęndan wv. *fundere, infundere, mittere*, ind. pres. 1 pl. asendað 21.7; ascendað 117.12; 3 pl. asendað 39.7; imp. sg. asynd 1.5; 46.9; asænd 116.14; pp. asænd 37.9; asend 116.6.

āsindrigan wv. *removere, segregare*, ind. pret. 2 sg. asindrodest 69.6; imp. sg. asyndra 53.14; pres. p. nsm. asyndrigende 133.14; nsn. asendrigende 6.8; pp. dsm. asindrodum 29.14; dpn. asindrodū 70.5; apf. asindrode 142.7.

āslīdan sv. *labascere, labi*, opt. pres. 3 sg. aslide 15.2; pp. dpm. aslidenum 7.6.

āsolcen adj. (pp.) *deses*, vpm. asolcene 19.2.

āspyrigend sm. *investigator*, ns. aspyrigend 33.12.

āstīgan sv. *ascendere, conscendere, scandere*, ind. pres. 2 sg. astihst 88.14; pret. 3 sg. astah 38.4; 70.6; 87.4; 89.4; 95.1; opt. pres. 2 sg. astige 80.3; 3 pl. astigan 113.17; inf. astigan 88.4; 116.4; 136.20; 139.12; astigen 90.6; pres. p. nsm. astigende 90.12.

āstręccan wv. *expandere, extendere*, ind. pres. 1 pl. astreccað 98.13; pres. p. nsm. astreccende 70.5.

āstyrigan wv. *excitare*, pp. nsm. astyred 6.9; nsf. astyrod 57.9.

āswindan sv. *torpere*, ind. pres. 3 sg. aswint 23.13.

ātēorigan wv. *fatiscere*, opt. pres. 3 sg. ateorige 24.4.

aðęnigan wv. *tendere*, pres. p. nsm. aðenigende 78.6.

aðinnian wv. *tenuare*, pp. aðinnod 8.10.

aðracigan wv. *abhorrere, horrere*, ind. pret. 3 sg. aðracude 51.4; pres. p. nsf. aðracigende 142.16.

aðrētnyss sf. *fastidium, taedium*, as. aðretnysse 25.12; aðrytnysse 6.4; æðrytnesse 133.14.

aðwēan sv. *lavare*, opt. pret. 3 sg. aðwoge 78.11; pp. nsm. aðwogen 51.12; 52.20; 54.4.

attor sn. *venenum*, ap. attru 16.8.

āwǣndan wv. *evertere, mutare, vertere*, ind. pret. 3 sg. awænde(?); imp. sg. awend 23.4; pres. p. nsf. awændende 76.17; pp. asn. awend 91.6.

āwęccan wv. *excitare, resuscitare, suscitare*, ind. pres. 3 sg. awecð 6.18; pret. 2 sg. awehtest 32.12; pres. p. nsm. aweccende 52.14.

āweggewītan sv. *abesse, abscedere, absistere, discedere, recedere*, ind. pres. 3 sg. aweggewit 1.4; 9.13; opt. pres. 3 sg. aweggewite 5.3; 9.10; 30.4; 3 pl. aweggewitan 11.14; imp. pl. aweggewitað 21.12.

āweorpan sv. *abjicere*, pp. dpn. aworpenum 108.12.

āwēstan wv. *devastare*, pres. p. dsm. awestendum 82.10.

āwrītan sv. *scribere*, opt. pres. 3 sg. awrite 114.12.

āwyrged adj. (ptc.) *malignus*, apf. awyrgede 47.12.

āwyrtwaligan wv. *radicare*, opt. pres. 3 sg. awyrtwalige 28.2.

āyrnan sv. *currere, decurrere*, opt. pres. 3 sg. ayrne 24.11; pp. áurnen 121.1; gsf. aurnenre (*declivi*), 36.4.

B

bænd, see bend.

balcettan wv. *eructare*, inf. 97.9.

bān sn. *os*, ap. bana 136.5.

be prep. w. dat. *de, ex, per*, 28.11; 79.12; 103.3; 106.6; 125.14; 129.3.

bearn sn. *filius, natus, partus, proles*, nvs. bearn 27.6; 73.12; 89.10; 93.13; 99.9; 139.1; 145.11; 146.10; gs. bearnes 103.10; ds. bearne 133.18; 139.17; dp. bearnum 99.5.

bebēodan sv. *jubere, praecipere*, ind. pres. 2 sg. bebeotst 13.17; bebeodst 49.9; 3 sg. bebeot 21.3; pres. p. gsm. bebeodendes 28.10.

becēpan wv. *vindicare*, opt. pres. 3 pl. becepan 120.17.

beclȳsan wv. *claudere*, ind. pres. 2 sg. beclyst 106.2; 124.12; 3 sg. beclysð 3.1; 2 pl. beclysað 122.9; pp. nsm. beclysed 51.2; 85.3; beclesed 31.9.

becuman sv. *effluere, occurrere, pervenire*, ind. pret. 3 sg. becom 134.8; opt. pres. 3 sg. becume 30.11; 114.6.

bedǣlan wv. *exuere*, pp. bedæled 3.9.

bedd sn. *cubile, lectulus*, ds. bedde 14.11; 26.5; 103.8; ap. bedd 19.1.

bedyppan wv. *tingere*, inf. 104.7.

befōn rv. *accingere, capere, cingere*, ind. pres. 3 sg. befehð 37.14; 111.7; inf. befon 44.14.

befȳlan wv. *foedare*, ind. pret. 3 sg. befylde 126.12.

begēman wv. *attendere, gubernare, intendere*, ind. pres. 3 sg. begymð 137.15; opt. pres. 3 sg. begeme 16.5; 127.7; imp. sg. begém 13.5; 22.2; 26.3; 39.7; 67.3; pres. p. nsm. begemende 143.2.

bēgen num. *ambo*, nom. begen 38.10; gen. begra 93.12.

begerdan wv. *accingere*, imp. sg. begerde 29.13.

begietan sv. *exsequi, quaesere*, ind. pret. 3 pl. begeaton 38.14; imp. sg. begyt 126.2; pp. nsm. begeten 28.1.

begleddigan wv. *illinere*, pp. npn. begleddode 22.3.

behāt sn. *promissum, volum*, gs. behates 92.11; 103.4; ds. behate 68.4; as. behát 139.4; ap. behát 7.14; 69.3; 105.19; 111.14; 124.10; 140.4; 141.3.

behātan rv. *promittere*, ind. pret. 3 sg. behét 93.13; pp. dsf. behatenre 95.3.

behealdan rv. *cernere, respicere*, ind. pres. 2 sg. behehealdst 7.9; 2 pl. behealde 87.10; imp. sg. beheald 7.7.

behēfnyss sf. *commodum*, ap. behefnyssa 5.11; 114.5.

behrēowsung sf. *poenitentia*, ds. behreowsunge 64.10.

behȳdan wv. *condere*, pp. behydd 7.5.

belūcan sv. *claudere*, pp. helocen (?).

bēn sf. *precatus, prex, oraculum, oratio, praeconium, supplicatio, quaestus, votum*, ns. ben 19.7; gs. bene 133.11; ds. bene 49.7; 72.12; 109.12; 111.15; 134.13; as. bene 77.4; dp. benum 70.3; 118.15; 119.4; 119.12; 119.15; 121.1; 124.16; 127.6; 128.8; 128.12; 129.4; ap. bena 2.10; 4.9; 13.19; 21.7; 34.9; 39.7; 46.9; 62.3; 67.3; 98.14; 99.1; 111.3; 113.11; 117.12; 122.8; 144.3; 146.13.

bend sm. *nexus, vinculum*, ds. bende 118.8; 134.4; bend 83.5; as. bænd 23.3; np. bendas 133.15; dp. bendum 32.3; 128.10; 133.17; ap. bendas 19.10; 29.1; 76.18; 80.1; 103.19; 120.15; 124.10.

beofigan wv. *tremere, tremescere*, ind. pret. 3 sg. beofode 32.10; 48.18.

bēon anv. *esse*, ind. pres. 1 sg. eom 19.4; 2 sg. eart (twenty-four times); 3 sg. is 8.10; 21.13; 43.6; 47.4; 65.17; 82.13; 84.

14; 87.11; 90.11; 96.12; 108.8; 108.10; 117.5; 135.16; 135. 17; 142.91; ys 37.9; 39.13; 40.1; 55.11; 58.2; 60.1; 60.2; 61.10; 73.3; 85.18; 89.12; 90. 14; 122.13; 141.10; 142.4; bið 7.4; 121.1; 130.22; 136.10; 136. 11; byð 7.5; 7.10; 51.9; 136. 9; 1 pl. beoð 5.8; 43.11; 126. 3; synt 40.5; 3 pl. beoð 22.4; 73.8; 133.2; 137.7; 137.8; synt 22.3; 35.2; 82.18; 132.5; 133. 15; sint 78.13; pret. 2 sg. wære 30.15; 32.6; 32.22; 3 sg. wæs (seventeen times); 1 pl. wæron 32.3; 3 pl. wæron 94.3; 94.9; 97. 1; 132.13; wæran 85.11; opt. pres. 2 sg. beo 14.17; 32.18; sy 11.13; 15.6; 76.10; 76.14; 79.11 (2); 98.3; 110.5; 146.8; 146.9; 3 sg. sy (fifty-four times); si 3.17; 5.21; 34.5; 45.17; 46.1; 63.8; 1 pl. beon 29.18; 36.13; 36. 16; 137.11; 3 pl. beon 9.9; 11. 17; 23.12; 29.13; 36.8; 63.6; 124.16; 143.6; 146.14; imp. sg. beo 88.9; 91.21; inf. beon 10. 3; 13.17; 20.9; 42.20; 54.8; 62.14; 73.9; 77.3; 77.6; 116. 6; 119.12; 120.13; 123.6; 125. 1; 125.3; wesan 103.1.

beorht adj. *clarus, splendidus,* nsmf. 37.1; 38.2; 47.3; 65. 16; dsn. byrhtum (?); dsf. beorhtre 86.7; asm. beorhtne 11.5; asn. beorht 53.11; dpm. beorhtū 136.4; apm. beorhte 47.10; apn. beorht 55.2.

beorhtnyss sf. *candor, claritas, nitor, splendor,* nvs. 5.1; 15.8; 114.15; 135.4; beortnyss 35.7; ds. beorhtnysse 15.13; beorhtnyssa 10.12; 22.9. See **bryhtnyss**.

beran sv. *ferre, gestare, portare,* ind. pres. 1 pl. beorað 32.16; pret. 3 pl. bæran 75.6; opt. pres. 1 pl. beran 80.16; pret. 2 sg. bære 84.2; pres. p. nsm. berende 59.7; 79.10; npm. berende 48. 12.

berðen sf. *sarcina,* ds. berðene 126.13.

berȳpan wv. *vastare,* ind. pret. 3 pl. berypton 38.11.

besæncan wv. *demergere, mergere,* inf. besæncan 48.17; pp. apmn. besænctan 20.14; 25.5.

besārgung sf. *compassio,* ns. besargung 126.10.

besārigan wv. *condolere, dolere,* imp. sg. besariga 125.3; pres. p. nsm. besarigende 34.10.

bescēawære sm. *speculator,* ns. besceawære 24.15.

bescēawigan wv. *conspicere, prospicere,* ind. pres. 2 sg. besæawast (*sic*) 143.10; 3 sg. besceawað 24.17; pret. 3 sg. besceawede 47.5.

besoūfan sv. *deputare, tradere,* pres. p. nsm. bescufende 134.7; pp. npm. bescofene 130.7.

besēon sv. *aspicere, respicere,* imp. sg. beseoh 13.3; 20.12.

besmītan sv. *inquinare, polluere,* opt. pres. 3 sg. besmite 24.14; pp. gsm. besmitenys 102.3; npm. besmitene 11.17.

besmitennyss sf. *contagium,* ds. besmitennysse 26.15; 48.16; as. besmetennysse 133.13.

beswīcan sv. *decipere,* ind. pret. 3 sg. beswac 31.5.

betæcan wv. *tradere*, pp. ds. betæhtum 106.1; 124.11.

betwux prep. w. dat. *inter*, 73.9; 77.12; 140.5.

betwuxsendan wv. *interpolare*, opt. pres. 3 sg. betwuxsende 44. 19.

betwuxsettan wv. *interserere*, opt. pres. 3 sg. betwuxseue 28.16.

betyrnan wv. *voltare*. pp. dsm. betrndū 96.3.

bewēpan rv. *deflere*. pres. p. bewepende 52.4.

bewerigan wv. *defendere*, *tutare*, opt. pres. 2 sg. bewerige 83.10; imp. sg. bewere 12.10; 54.2; inf. bewerian 61.15.

bewerigend sm. *defensor*. nvs. 13. 3; 13.9.

bewindan sv. *obserere*, pp. asn. bewunden 48.10.

biddan sv. *adorare*, *depescere*, *deprecari*, *exorare*. *exposcere*. *flagitare*, *impetrare*, *orare*, *petere*, *poscere*. *postulare*, *precari*, *quaesere*, *rogare*, *rogitare*, *supplicare*. ind. pres. 1 pl. biddað 5.2; 5.9; 11.11; 12.9; 14.13; 15.3; 20. 15; 22.1; 23.7; 26.17; 33.19; 35.9; 47.11; 47.14; 49.8; 53. 9; 56.10; 59.9; 67.7; 68.3; 71. 1; 72.1; 80.11; 83.7; 91.13; 94. 14; 105.3; 108.11; 113.3; 119. 11; 122.7; 122.12; 124.5; 127. 12; 128.6; 131.1; 134.14; 136. 13; 140.13; 143.1; 144.5; 146. 17; opt. pres. 1 pl. biddan 26.7; 54.17; 127.9; 3 pl. biddan 1.7; 118.4; 118.16; imp. sg. bide 73. 10; 77.2; 117.16; 2 pl. biddað 106.10; 126.17; inf. biddan 3. 13; 8.12; 9.2; 111.17; 116.6;

pres. p. nsm. biddende 54.17; npm. biddende 19.6; 91.13; 113. 8; 120.12; gpm. biddendra 105. 19; 124.10; dpm. biddendum 18.4; 18.11; 126.7; apm. biddende 124.7; 131.3; biddendan 3.16.

bigenc sm. *cultor* vs. 104.10.

binn sf. *praesepe*, ns. binn 44.17; as. binne 51.4.

biscop sm. *pontifex*, *praesul*, gp. biscopa 98.3; 113.10; 137.18.

bisen sf. *exemplum*, ap. bisena 66. 10.

blācigan wv. *pallere*. pres. p. nsf. blacigende 24.4.

blācung sf. *pallor*, as. blacunge 35.6.

blādesigan wv. *flammescere*, opt. pres. 3 sg. bladesige 10.7.

blǣd sm. *flamen*. *flatus*. *spiramen*, ns. blæd 73.13; ds. blæde 43. 18; 74.6.

blēoh sn. *color*, ns. bleoh 21.15; ap. bleoh 23.6.

blind adj. *caecus*, *orbatus*, dpm. blindum 76.19; 136.11; 142.2.

blindnyss sf. *caecitas*, ns. blyndnyss 24.4.

bliss sf. *gaudium*, ap. blissa 91.12.

blissigan wv. *exultare*. *gaudere*, ind. pres. 3 sg. blissað 124.3; 130.21; pret. 3 pl. blissodon 96. 15; opt. pres. 3 sg. blissige 24. 1; 122.1; 1 pl. blissian 112.2; inf. blissigan 125.6; pres. p. nsm. blissigende 40.3; 84.16; gpm. blissigendra 56.1.

blīðe adj. *laetus*, nsmf. bliðe 16. 13; 55.14; 136.19; 138.10; npm. 16.11; 56.14; 143.6; dpm. bliðum 57.9; 123.11; 129.12.

blōd sn. *sanguis*, ns. blod 130.12; gs. blodes 25.10; 141.12; ds. blode 13.6; 32.20; 40.5; 49.1; 78.12; 80.12; 82.7; 125.5; 133. 1; 139.11; as. blod 32.7; 134. 11.

blōdig adj. *sanguineus*, apm. blodige 47.9.

blōsm sm. *flos*, ds. blosme 132.6; dp. blosmum 19.18.

blōwan sv. *florere*, pres. p. npf. blowende 135.9.

bōc sf. *liber*, ds. béc 114.14.

bodigan wv. *praecinere*, *praedicare*, ind. pres. 3 sg. bodaŏ 18.14; 3 pl. bodiaŏ 74.17; pret. 3 pl. bodeden 135.10; pres. p. nsm. bodiende 12.8; bodigende 74.8.

bodung sf. *praeconium*, *nuntius*, ds. bodunge 36.7; 75.15.

bōg sm. *stipes*, ds. boge 79.1.

borhgelda wm. *debitor*, dp. borhgeldum 33.1.

bōsm sm. *gremium*, ds. bosme 121.2.

brēce sm. *usus*, ds. brece 143.12.

brēd sf. *sponsa*, ap. breda 140.7. See **brȳdguma**.

brēdbūr sn. *thalamus*, ds. bredbure 34.15; 44.5; 103.9.

brēman wv. *celebrare*, ind. pres. 3 sg. brymŏ 138.5; 3 pl. bremaŏ 143.3; 105.1; opt. pres. 3 sg. breme 48.4; 57.14; 58.11; pret. 3 sg. brymde 136.18. See **brȳme**.

brēost sn. *pectus*, gs. breostes 36. 10; 50.13; 104.17; 108.6; 139. 16; ds. breoste 10.4; 61.2; 72. 4; 75.22; gp. breosta 33.11; 61.15; ap. breost 27.18; 36.5;

92.4; 96.13; breosta 113.15; breoste 93.7; 94.17; 96.9; 97. 5; 98.1.

bringan wv. *afferre, deferre, ferre*, ind. pret. 3 sg. brohte 30.8; 52. 9; 75.8; 94.2; opt. pres. 3 sg. bringe 17.14; imp. sg. bring 109.3.

brōŏor sm. *frater, germanus*, ns. broŏor 38.6; vs. broŏer 126.9.

brūcan sv. *frui, perfrui, potiri*, ind. pres. 3 sg. brucŏ 138.10; 3 pl. brucaŏ 136.4; opt. pres. 1 pl. brucan 73.17; 128.12; 129.8; brucon 29.10; pres. p. nsm. brucende 133.10.

brȳdguma wm. *sponsus*, ns. 34.15; 112.10; dp. bredgumū 140.8. See **brēd**, **brēdbūr**.

bryhtnyss sf. *splendor*, ns. 39.5. See **beorhtnyss**.

brym sm. *aequor, fretum, pontus*, ns. 74.18; ds. brymme 70.16; np. brymmas 6.14; ap. brymmas 38.11.

brȳme adj. *celeber*, nsm. bryme 38.2. See **brēman**.

brynan, see **byrnan**.

bryne sm. *ardor*, ns. 10.3; 26. 16.

burh sf. *urbs*, ns. 57.8.

burhlēode sfpl. *cives*, dp. burhleodum 112.1.

burne wf. *latex*, ns. 103.18; ds. burnan 70.15; np. burnan 141.13.

būtan prep. w. dat. *sine*, 47. 16; 145.5.

bydel sm. *nuntius, praeco*, nvs. 6. 5; 18.13; 102.5; 110.2; 129.1.

byrgen sf. *tumulus*, ds. byrgene 83.3; 137.5.

byrnan sv. *ardere, flagrare, flammescere*, opt. pres. 3 sg. byrne 114.4; bryne 10.7; pres. p. nsmn. byrnende 27.9; 70.7.

C

cǣgbora sm. *claviger*, ns. cǣgbora 118.6.

cænnan wv. *parturire*, ind. pret. 3 sg. cænde 75.10.

cæstergewara wm. *civis, concivis*, ns. 55.15; np. cæstergewaran 57.2; cæstergewara 118.14; cæstergewaru 105.1; gp. 56.1; 103.13; dp. cæstergewarum 46.14.

cafertūn sm. *atrium*, as. cafertun 135.7.

cāflice adv. *naviter*, caflice 57.2.

cēast sfn. *lis*, gp. ceasta 10.14.

cempa wm. *miles*, ds. cæmpan (?); gp. cempena 134.1; ap. cempan 115.4; vp. cempan 123.14; 130.1.

cenehelm, see cynehelm.

cennestre, see cynnestre.

cenning sf. *partus*, ds. cenninge 54.11.

ceorung sf. *quaerimonia*, ns. 132.14.

cīdan wv. *arguere*, ind. pres. 3 sg. cit 7.2.

cīgan, see cīon.

cild smn. *parvulus, puer, puerulus*, gs. cildes 70.1; as. cild 48.9; 70.14.

cildclāð sm. *pannus*, dat. eildclāðū 48.10.

cildcradel sm. *cunabula*, ds. cildcradele 48.8.

cildlic adj. *juvenilis*, apm. cildlice 70.7.

cing, see cyng.

cīon wv. *ciere, invocare, vocare*, ind. pres. 1 pl. ciað 15.16; 117.9; 144.5; inf. cion 19.5. See gecīgan.

clǣne adj. *castus, mundus, purus, pudicus*, nsmf. clæne 2.15; 42.19; 108.7; 137.2; gsn. clænes 50.13; 52.7; 139.15; dsmn. clænum 21.18; 61.2; 72.4; 141.5; dsf. clænre 29.9; 68.3; 70.8; 115.12; dsm. clænan 16.6; 42.15; asfn. clæne 19.8; 77.7; vsn. clæne 27.6; npn. clæne 9.9; dpn. clænum 104.21; apm. clæne 24.8; 50.9; 77.14; clænan 3.7; vpm. clæne 19.3; sup. gpm. clænnestra 113.9.

clǣnnyss sf. *castitas, pudicitia, pudor*, ns. clænnyss 16.14; clænnys 118.11; gs. clænnysse 44.2; 61.18; 104.9; clænnyssa 44.6.

clāwu sf. *ungula*, dp. clawum 130.9.

cleopigan wv. *clamare*, ind. pres. 3 sg. cleopað 19.1; 85.10; pres. p. gpm. cleopigendra (?).

clēsing, see clȳsing.

clincig adj. *asper*, asn. clincig 104.18.

clūse wf. *claustrum*, ap. clusan 61.15.

clypung wf. *invocatio*, ns. 1.1.

clȳsing sf. *clausa, claustrum, clausula*, ns. clysing 44.2; 75.2; 112.7; ds. clysinga 34.17; ap. clesinga 84.5.

cnēow sn. *genu*, ns. cneow 108. 10; as. cneow 91.4; np. cneowe 35.2.

cnyssan wv. *pellere*, opt. pres. 3 sg. cnysse 14.5.

cocc sm. *gallus*, ns. 7.2.

cræft sm. *machina*, ns. 91.1; gs. cræftes 29.4; as. 75.1; 137.15.

cræftiga wm. *artifex*, ns. cræfeca 75.12.

cræt sn. *currus*, ds. cræte 66.4.

crāwan rv. *canere*, pres. p. dsm. crawendum 6.16; crawendan 7.3.

crisma wm. *chrisma*, gs. crisman 87.6; ds. crisman 141.15.

Crist sm. *Christus*, nvs. crist 12. 5; 16.9; 18.9; 18.16; 19.9; 20. 15; 21.12; 21.17; 23.11; 34.8; 35.9; 37.4; 39.1; 42.1; 49.7; 57. 14; 58.11; 60.2; 65.18; 69.1; 71.1; 72.6; 79.17; 82.13; 83.3; 86.15; 87.3; 89.3; 91.9; 95.1; 97.15; 108.8; 114.15; 115.10; 115.17; 116.1; 119.1; 120.11; 123.4; 124.13; 126.8; 132.8; 135.4; 135.17; 138.15; 141.1; 145.11; gs. cristes 3.14; 61.8; 66.8; 86.12; 96.13; 97.10; 106. 15; 112.4; 118.5; 120.2; 120. 5; 123.8; 123.18; 129.9; 130. 17; 136.6; crist 128.5; ds. criste 45.3; 45.7; 45.9; 45.11; 45.13; 45.15; 50.3; 52.6; 59.4; 73.4; 77.16; 82.4; 99.1; as. crist 3. 13; 12.2; 38.13; 51.14; 54.16; 86.9; 90.4; 129.3.

cristen adj. *christicola*, gpm. cristenra 141.16.

cuman sv. *venire*, ind. pres. 3 sg. cymð 21.12; 38.2; pret. 3 sg. com 53.2; 95.2; 126.8; opt. pres. 3 sg. cume 116.11; 3 pl. cuman 116.7; pret. 2 sg. come 39.16; imp. sg. cum 43.13; 92.1; inf. cuman 51.14; 53.17; 73.3; 96.8; pres. p. nsm. cumende 102.5; 104.22; dsf. cumendre 108.11.

cunnan swv. *noscere, scire*, ind. pres. 1 pl. cunnon 4.8; 21.17; 53.17; 93.3; pret. 3 sg. cuðe 50.12; opt. pres. 3 sg. cunne (?).

cuð adj. *certus, cognitus*, nsm. cuð 74.9; asf. cuðe 33.15.

cwalu sf. *nex*, ds. cwale 85.12.

cwellære sm. *tortor*, gs. cwellæres 130.10.

cwēn sf. *regina*, vs. cwén 111.1.

cweðan sv. *inquam*, ind. pret. 3 pl. cwædon 87.11.

cwicsūsl sf. *barathrum*, as. cwicsusle 128.3.

cwide sm. *dictum*, ds. cwidu 28. 10.

cwild sn. *pestis*, np. cwild 99.7.

cwilmigan wv. *cruciare*, opt. pres. 3 pl. cwylmige 143.5; inf. cwilmigan 70.6.

cynedōm sm. *imperium*, ns. cynedom 106.13; 125.8.

cynegyrd sf. *sceptrum*, as. 54.1.

cynehelm sm. *corona, sertum*, vs. cynehelm 134.2; 140.1; cenehelm 131.6; 137.18; np. cynehelmas 104.12; ap. cynehelmas 91.20.

cynelic adj. *regius*, vsn. cynelic 108.2; dsf. cynelic 44.6.

cynesetl sn. *solium*, ds. cynesetle 128.9.

cyng sm. *rex*, nvs. 86.15; 90.8; 112.6; 115.10; 125.6; 136.8; 138.15; cing 84.18; gs. cynges 76.5; 78.1; 78.18; 142.10; ds. cyninge 8.1; 45.3; as. cynge 103.9; vs. 30.13; 131.5.

cynn sn. *genus*, ns. 48.3; 112.8; 141.15; gs. cynnes 31.6; 116.2; as. 25.2; 28.8; 52.15; 132.4; ap. 139.10.

cynnestre wf. *genitrix*, ns. cynnystre 116.17; ds. cynnestran 54.7; vs. cynnestra 117.15; cennestre 55.11.

cynren sn. *stirps*, gs. cynrenes 108.2; ds. cynrene 25.7.

cystiglice adv. *large*, comp. cystiglicor 29.10; 140.13.

cȳðan wv. *nuntiare*, ind. pres. 3 sg. cȳð 27.12.

cȳðere sm. *martyr*, ds. cȳðere 45.2; 45.4; 46.2. See forma cȳðere.

D

dǣd sf. *actus, factum, gestum*, ns. dǣd 5.4; ds. dǣde 5.13; as. dǣde 20.10; gp. dǣda 14.16; 102. 2; dp. dǣdum 9.3; 21.4; 27.2; 28.16; 90.3; ap. dǣda 16.1; 20. 5; 24.17; 36.10; 116.16; 132.2.

dæg sm. *dies*, nvs. 9.13; 12.5; 15. 11; 16.13; 18.2; 24.11; 30.2; 38.1; 39.13; 47.3; 47.5; 61.11; 89.2; 96.1; 117.6; 143.9; gs. dæges 4.14; 6.5; 18.13; 27.17; 145.3; ds. dæge 2.9; 4.1; 22. 11; 40.6; 105.13; 138.1; as. 2.3; 3.2; 6.2; 13.17; 60.4; np. dagas 143.6; gp. dagena 4.1;

13.13; 15.11; 94.11; dægena 27.1; dp. dægum 24.16.

dægrima wm. *aurora*, ns. 8.11; 16.17; 84.14.

dægsteorra wm. *Lucifer*, ns. dægsteorra 27.11; dægsteorre 6.9.

dægðerlic adj. *diurnus*, gsn. dægðerlices 11.3; dp. dægðerlicum 9.3; 14.19.

dǣl sm. *pars*, ds. dǣle 48.14; 106.6; 125.14.

dǣlmǣlum adv. *partim*, 25.3; 25.4.

dara sf. *noxa*, ns. 24.14; as. dara 134.16; 138.14; ap. dara 15.4; 141.14.

Dauidlic adj. *Davidicus*, gsn. dauidlices 108.2.

dēad adj. *mortuus*, nsm. dead 45. 10; 111.11; gpm. deadra 136. 5; dpm. deadum 83.12; 136. 10.

dēadlic adj. *mortalis*, gpm. deadlicra 27.4; 91.6; apn. deadlice 51.15.

dēað sm. *mors*, ns. deað 90.10; gs. deaðes 11.7; 20.10; 25.12; 31.8; 32.14; 33.1; 34.11; 80. 7; 83.9; 84.19; 85.13; 112. 14; 125.2; 130.5; 139.9; ds. deaðe 4.4; deaþe 53.7; 79.14; 80.5; 84.4; 106.10; 111.10; as. deað 38.15; 45.12; 139.9; deaþ 79.13; 80.5; 84.3.

dēg sf. *fucus*, dp. degū 22.3.

dēma wm. *judex*, nvs. dema 23. 8; 33.7; 35.10; 36.9; 123.3; gs. deman 91.18; 119.9; 127. 10; nvp. deman 105.15; 122.5.

dēman wv. *censere*, ind. pret. 3 sg. demde 21.4.

dēoful sm. *daemon, diabolus, Pharao, zabulus*, ns. deoful 31.5; gs. deofles 82.12; 142.5; as. deoful 80.8; 115.8; gp. deofla 18.6; 26.9; 125.1.

dēop adj. *altus, profundus*, gsf. deopre 6.6; dpn. deopū 28.2.

dēopnyss sf. *altum, profundum*, ds. deopnysse 3.1; np. deopnyssa 3.10.

deore adj. *obscurus*, asf. deorce 53.14.

dēorwurðe adj. *pretiosus*, vsm. deorwurðe 46.3.

derigan wv. *laedere, nocere*, ind. pres. 3 sg. derað 142.15; ger. to derigenne 6.12.

derigendlic adj. *nocens, noxius*, nsnf. derigendlic 5.4; 23.14; gsn. derigendlices 14.7; 37.8; 93.2; dsf. derigendlicre 20.13; asf. derigendlice 10.15; npn. derigendlice 99.7; dpm. derigendlicū 9.4; apnf. derigendlice 133.4; 134.6.

dīgol adj. *abditus, obstrusus* [i. e. *abstrusus*], *occultus, secretus*, dsn. diglum 103.8; dpn. dyglum 36.11; apn. diglu 21.6; 139.11; diglo 136.19; diglan 33.9.

digolnyss sf. *abditum, secretum*, ap. digolnyssa 103.11; digelnysse 50.12.

dimnyss sf. *caligo*, ns. 3.2; 27.13; dymnes 21.13; ds. dymnisse 6.10; as. dymnesse 23.17.

dōmsetl sn. *tribunal*, as. domsetl 90.12.

dōn anv. *agere, facere, gerere, reddere*, ind. pres. 1 pl. doð 106.6; 125.14; pret. 3 sg. dede 126.11; 1 pl. dedon 21.5; opt. pres. 2 sg. do 47.12; 3 sg. do 2.6; 123.6; imp. sg. do 49.14; 77.14; 125.6; pl. doð 120.2; inf. don 89.13; 145.2; ger. to donne 16.4; 21.3.

drēam sm. *canor, modulus, organum*, ns. dream 58.2; ds. dreame 30.12; ap. dreamas 103.5; 103.7.

drēfende adj. (ptc.) *turbidus*, apn. drefende 127.3.

drēman wv. *modulari*, opt. pres. 3 sg. dreme 141.19.

drenc sm. *haustus, poculum, potus*, ns. drenc 16.10; 58.5; gs. drences 9.12; as. drenc 31.8; 103.18; 141.12.

drencfæt sn. *poculum*, ap. drencfatu 112.14.

Drihten sm. *Dominus*, nvs. 12.9; 13.7; 13.10; 30.13; 32.12; 33.5; 40.8; 40.12; 42.1; 43.12; 44.21; 46.12; 51.11; 52.19; 53.13; 54.3; 60.7; 76.9; 83.11; 84.13; 85.9; 85.17; 86.19; 88.13; 90.7; 91.22; 112.3; 124.13; 125.7; 136.13; gs. drihtnes 38.15; 54.14; 73.1; 85.12; 86.2; 86.6; 109.1; 119.10; 126.9; 136.17; drihtnys 61.14; ds. drihtne 7.18; 45.1; 57.12; 70.11; 87.1; 113.12; as. 12.2; 43.10; 46.7; 54.9; 86.13; 111.4.

drihtwurðe adj. *theologus*, vsm. 126.6.

drincan sv. *bibere*, ind. pres. 3 sg. drincð 141.11; inf. 16.11.

drohtnigan wv. *degere, versari,* ind. pres. 3 sg. drohtnað 44.4; 1 pl. drohniað 113.8.

druncennyss sf. *ebrietas,* as. druncennisse 16.12.

druncnigan wv. *madere,* inf. 94.7.

dūn sm. *mons,* dp. dunan 87.6.

dūst sn. *pulvis,* gs. dustes 136.1.

dȳgol, see dīgol.

dymness, see dimnyss.

E

ēa sf. *flumen,* ds. ea 51.12.

ēac swilce conj. *et, nec non, quoque,* eac swilce 27.8; 40.4; 42. 14; 90.9; 119.5; 126.6; 133.5; 145.2; 146.2; eac swylce 98.8.

ēadig adj. *beatus,* nvsmnf. eadig 27.4; 50.5; 75.11; 75.15; 79. 3; 139.5; 144.6; nvsf. eadige 1.2; 8.5; 56.11; 63.4; 80.17; 117.2; gsmn. eadiges 29.17; 119.3; 141.11; dsn. eadigum 24.1; asn. eadig 8.3; 12.8; 130. 6; vsm. eadige 128.1; dpmf. eadigum 4.16; 36.15; 121.1; apmf. eadige 70.9; 96.4; apf. eadiga 93.16; vpn. eadige 119. 5; sup. vsn. eadigosta 110.9.

ēadmōd adj. *cernuus, humilis, pronus, supplex,* nvsmn. eadmod 1.8; 137.1; 141.6; dsm. eadmodum 47.14; 94.14; dsf. eadmodre 49.7; 134.13; npm. eadmode 15.3; 30.10; 47.11; 111.17; 117.9; 117.11; 127.9; eadmod 105.3; gpm. eadmodra 34.9; 69.3; 110.12; 118.15; 141.3; eadmoddra 122.8.

ēadmōdlic adj. *supplex,* npm. eadmodlice 9.2.

ēadmōdlice adv. *suppliciter,* eadmodlice 119.11.

ēage wn. *lumen, oculus,* ds. eagan 54.16; np. eagan 12.17; 24.13.

ēahðerl sn. *fenestra,* ns. eahðerl 76.4.

ēalā interj. *O,* eala (131 times).

eald adj. *antiquus, senex, vetitus, vetus,* nsn. 17.12; nsm. ealde 54.13; gsmn. ealdan 31.7; 32.13; asf. calde 19.11; asm. ealdan 116.10; apm. ealdan 141.13.

ealdor sm. *auctor, primas, princeps,* nvs. 38.7; 39.9; 50.5; 69.2; 79.15; 83.7; 116.2; gs. ealdres 38.6; ds. ealdre 30.3; 82.4; 89.6; as. 40.2; 115.5; 123.19; 130.18; vp. ealdres 123.12; 129.13.

ealdorlic adj. *principalis,* vsf. 1.3.

eall adj. *cunctus, omnis, totus,* [ealra swiðost 23.18 = *quam maxime*], ns. 16.18; 16.19; 16. 20; 24.11; 32.10; 40.1; 43. 15; 48.3; 74.11; 108.9; 111.7; 117.1; 117.3; gsm. ealles 137. 15; dsmn. callum 8.7; 47.4; 60.12; asm. ealne 111.5; asnf. ealle 14.8; 105.11; asf. 80.15; npmnf. ealle 4.6; 7.16; 8.12; 29. 18; 35.2; 37.11; 43.2; 47.11; 49.8; 72.5; 75.3; 116.8; 118.1; 118.14; 145.8; 145.18; 146.1; gp. ealra (thirty-two times); dp. callum (twenty times); apmnf. ealle 1.9; 3.15; 15.4; 17.15; 28.6; 34.3; 53.4; 59.15; 77. 2; 88.12; 108.4; 108.16; 114.

7; 115.4; 116.14; 142.12; 145.
7; apmf. ealla 49.17; 68.12;
128.7; 133.6; 140.15.

eallunga adv. *jam, penitus, prorsus*, 1.4; 2.9; 5.1; 9.1; 18.16;
21.15; 28.1; 30.1; 31.14; 37.
5; 44.17; 47.3; 48.14; 58.1;
63.3; 82.13; 85.7; 86.9; 95.1;
132.7; 140.15.

ealneweg adv. *jugiter*, 43.11;
113.7.

earc sf. *arca*, ds. earce 75.14.

ēare wn. *auris*, ds. earan 75.9; as.
care 131.9; ap. earan 127.10.

earm sm. *brachium, ulna*, dp.
earmum 57.13; 79.3.

earming sm. *miser*, dp. earming-
um 117.16; 126.8; ap. eorming-
as 85.2.

ēasterlic adj. *paschalis*, dsf. easter-
licre 86.7; easterlican 83.8;
apnf. easterlice 65.9; 68.7.

ēasterne adj. *Eous*, gsn. easternes
22.5.

Ēastre wf. *Pascha*, gs. eastran
82.9; 94.10; as. castran 56.13;
82.13.

ēce adj. *aeternus, immensus, perennis, perpes, sempiternus*, nvsmnf.
ece 6.1; 11.8; 27.3; 30.13;
34.7; 39.6; 55.5; 55.9; 57.3;
57.10; 57.13; 57.16; 58.3; 58.
7; 58.10; 74.13; 90.8; 105.6;
106.11; 127.8; 134.17; 137.
18; 145.13; 146.5; 146.9;
gsn. eces 5.11; 15.17; 57.5;
105.6; 130.14; gsf. ccere 17.10;
gsm. ecan 55.1; 109.2; 119.
9; 141.2; 142.10; dsn. ecum
121.3; dsf. ecere 15.13; 44.16;
92.16; dsm. ecan 44.13; 59.2;

asmn. ece 57.7; 116.3; 143.10;
npm. ece 36.16; dpm. ecum 123.
5; apnf. ece 35.16; 40.11; 43.
4; 47.2; 83.14; 106.14; 118.20;
120.10; 124.8; 131.4; 134.12;
vpn. ece 123.8; 129.9.

ēcelic adj. *perennis*, gsn. ecelices
14.3.

ēcelice adv. *per aevum, perenne,
perenniter, perpetim*, ecelice 29.
13; 49.17; 56.5; 56.15; 65.13;
112.1; 125.6.

ēcen adj. *fecundus*, vsnf. ecne 75.
16; 79.9.

ēcnyss sf. *aevum, perpetuum*, as.
ecnysse 1.13; 5.20; 15.6; 34.
4; ecnyssa 12.3; 136.18; 146.
7; ccnessa 59.16.

edstaðoligan wv. *restituere*, pp.
npm. edstaðolode 137.8.

edwist sf. *substantia*, gs. edwiste
44.7.

efel, see **yfel**.

efenēce adj. *comperennis*, nsn.
73.12.

efenhlytta wm. *consors*, nvs.
efenhlytta 18.1; 38.8; vs. efen-
lytta 42.4; np. yfenlyttan 120.2.

efne interj. *ecce*, 8.10; 23.13; 24.
3; 37.1; 38.1.

ęfstan wv. *tendere*, opt. pres. 1
pl. efstan 65.9; inf. efstan 88.6.

ęft adv. *item*, 53.18.

ęge sm. *timor*, ns. ege 142.3.

ęgeslic adj. *horrendus*, gsm.
egeslican 47.12.

Egyptaland sn. *Aegyptus*, ds.
egypto lande 43.6.

ęlebēam sm. *oliva*, vp. elebeames
106.7.

embhegigan wv. *saepire*, pp. nsm. emhegod 140.6.

embhwerft sm. *orbis*, ns. 74. 11; 108.9; gs. embhwerftes 104.4; 105.14; ds. embhwerfte 36.3; 65.17; 96.3; as. embhwerft 26.2; 38.10; 39.8; 73.7; 136.18.

embryne, see ymbryne.

embscrȳdan wv. *induere*, ind. pret. 3 sg. embscredde 50.6.

embtrymmung sf. *munimen*, ds. emtrymminge 136.14; ap. emtrymnunga 146.19.

ende, see ænde.

endebyrdnyss, see ændebyrdnyss.

eugel, see ængel.

engelic, see ængelic.

eorendel sm. *Aurora*, ns. 16.18; 30.1.

eorming, see earming.

eornostlice adj. *ergo*, 6.17; 33. 19; 49.3; 59.9; 61.14; 68.5; 75.7; 89.13; 96.11; 143.1.

eorðe wf. *tellus*, *terra*, ns. 32. 10; 39.17; 74.16; 122.2; gs. eorðan 17.6; 17.8; 19.13; 21. 13; 23.6; 50.2; 54.9; 97.17; as. eorðan 19.16; dp. eorðū 30. 2; ap. eorðan 45.15.

eorðlic adj. *terrenus*, *terrestris*, npn. eorðlice 35.3; gpn. eorðlicra 91.2; apn. eorðlice 131.7.

ēowde sn. *grex*, ds. eowde 73.5.

ēower poss. prn. *vester*, dpf. eowrum 119.12; 119.15.

ēstfull adj. *devotus*, nsmn. estfull 113.12; 123.16; 138.6; nsm.

estful 130.15; dsn. estfullum 31.20; 46.9; 110.12; asn. estfull 70.1; dpn. estfullum 145.1; apm. estfulle 106.8; apf. estfullan 67.4.

ēstfullic adj. *devotus*, npm. estfullice 146.2.

ēstfulnyss sf. *devotio*, ds. estfulnysse 88.6.

etan sv. *edere*, inf. 60.3.

ēðel smn. *patria*, gs. eðeles 29. 17; 58.1; as. eðel 142.11.

ēðigan wv. *spirare*, ind. pres. 3 sg. eðað 44.18.

F

fācen sn. *dolus*, *fraus*, gs. facnes 16.8; facnyss 17.11; ds. facne 3.11; 26.9; 125.1.

fācenfull adj. *subdolus*, asm. facenfulne 80.7.

fācenfullic adj. *subdolus*, gsn. facenfullices 24.9.

fæc sn. *spatium*, as. 104.4.

fæder sm. *parens*, *pater*, nvs. (twenty-three times); gs. fæderes 3.14; 8.6; 10.2; 39.2; 39.5; 39.15; 45.5; 49.4; 73.11; 80. 9; 87.4; 89.7; 90.13; 92.11; 95.3; 96.11; 109.2; 114.15; 133. 8; 141.2; fæder 8.16; 84.8; ds. (forty-two times); fædor 30.18; as. 3.13; 15.16; 15.17; 15.18; 52.12; 93.3; 141.17; dp. fæderum 73.1.

fæderlic adj. *paternus*, nsn. fæderlic 124.1; 130.19; gsn. fæderlices 15.8; 18.1; dsn. fæderlicum 89.12; asn. fæderlic 43. 3; vsf. fæderlice 5.1.

fægnigan wv. *gaudere, jubilare, plaudere,* ind. pres. 3 sg. fægnað 84.16; imp. pl. fægniað 76.8; pres. p. nsm. fægnigende 54.14.

fægnung sf. *jubilatio,* ns. 106.12.

fǣmne wf. *femina, virgo,* ds. fæmnan, 31.17; vs. fæmne 75.19.

færeld sn. *gressus,* as. 136.12; ap. færeldu 104.23.

fǣrlice adv. *repente,* færlice 50.14; 96.6.

fæst adj. *firmus,* nsf. 114.4.

fæstan wv. *jejunare,* opt. pres. 3 sg. fæste 63.2.

fæsten sn. *jejunium,* gs. fæstenes 65.16; ds. fæstene 62.4; as. 64.4; 68.8; gp. fæstena 63.7; 65.8.

fæsthafol adj. *tenax,* nsf. 11.1.

fæt sn. *lucerna,* as. 74.14.

feala adj. *multus,* npn. 22.3.

feallan rv. *cadere, concidere, decidere,* ind. pres. 3 sg. fealð 27.13; 3 pl. feallað 7.9; opt. pres. 3 sg. fealle 11.6; 25.15; 30.5; 30.8; pres. p. npm. feallende 48.9.

fēdan wv. *pascere,* ind. pres. 2 sg. fetst 140.5.

feohtan sv. *pugnare,* ind. pres. 3 sg. feoht 135.15.

fēond sm. *hostis, inimicus,* nvs. feond 12.14; 31.6; 51.13; gs. feondes 3.11; 32.13; 35.12; 47.12; 115.11; 135.3; as. feond 11.16; 92.17; 113.13; 116.9; dp. feondum 133.9.

fēondlic adj. *inimicus,* dsn. feondlicum 46.7.

feor adv. *procul,* 4.5; 11.14; 115.9.

feorran adv. *eminus, longius,* 37.3; 92.17.

fēorða num. *quartus,* dsm. feorðan 22.11.

fēower num. *quaterni,* dpf. feower 61.10.

fēowertigfeald adj. *quadragenarius,* gsf. feowertigfealdre 64.1; dsn. feowertigum fealdum 62.5.

fēr, see **fȳr.**

fēran wv. *ire, petere,* ind. pret. 2 sg. ferdest 55.3; 3 pl. ferdan 51.17.

fēren, see **fȳren.**

ferwyt, see **fyrwit.**

fēst sf. *pugillus,* ds. feste 75.13.

finger sm. *digitus,* ns. 92.10.

fīr, see **fȳr.**

fiscere sm. *piscator,* ns. 38.9.

flǣsc sn. *caro,* ns. flæsc 12.15; 43.19; 82.16; 91.7; 91.8; gs. flæsces 5.13; 9.11; 31.16; 78.3; ds. flæsce 78.3.

flǣsclic adj. *carneus,* dsf. flæsclicre 42.19.

flān smf. *telum,* dp. flanū 35.12.

flēon sv. *fugere, volitare,* ind. pres. 3 sg. flihð 142.7; opt. pres. 3 sg. fleo 116.10.

flōd sn. *fluens, flumen,* ds. flode 48.18; ap. flod 17.3; 56.3.

flōwan rv. *effluere,* opt. pres. 3 sg. flowe 30.11; pres. p. (*fluidus*) dsn. flowendū 133.1.

fōda wm. *pastus*, as. fodan 20.2; 103.18.

folc sn. *plebs, populus*, ns. 83.1; 120.16; 136.18; 138.6; 141.6; 141.10; ds. folce 46.8; 135.10; 136.8; as. 83.10; dp. folcum 60.6.

folgigan wv. *sequi*, ind. pres. 3 pl. folgiað 140.10; pret. 3 pl. folgedon 38.15; opt. pret. 3 sg. folgode 69.8; pres. p. npm. folgiende 51.18.

for prep. w. dat. *pro*, 36.11; 36.12; 36.14; 37.11; 37.15; 40.6; 46.7; 46.9; 47.13; 65. 1; 77.5; 79.14; 80.4; 110. 11; 111.11; 111.20; 113.11; 132.9; 134.11; 136.2; 139. 13; *ob, propter*, w. acc. 32.5; 32.21; 64.3; w. inst. 5.9; 26.17; 54.15; 125.2; 134.13.

forbærnan wv. *adurere, perurere*, imp. sg. forbærn 29.12; pp. gsn. forbærndes 20.3.

forbēn sf. *precatus*, ds. forbene 138.13.

forbēodan sv. *vetare*, opt. pres. 3 sg. forbeode 19.8.

forberan sv. *ferre*, inf. 25.12.

forbūgan sv. *vitare*, opt. pres. 1 pl. forbugan 14.7; 93.2.

forceorfan sv. *conlidere*, pp. apn. forcorfene 52.4.

fordēman wv. *damnare*, ind. pret. 3 pl. fordemdan 85.14.

forebēon sn. *prodigium*, dp. forebecnum 74.7.

foregewissigan wv. *prodesse*, ind. pret. 3 sg. foregewissode 111.9.

foreglēaw adj. *providus*, gsn. foregleawes 82.1.

foreglēawlice adv. *provide*, forgleawlice 75.21.

foremihtig adj. *praepotens*, nvsm. 74.5; 104.10.

foresęcgan wv. *praedicere*, ind. pret. 3 sg. foresæde 50.18; 85. 16.

forestæppan sv. pres. p. (*praevius*) nvsm. 98.6; 118.5; foresteppende 48.7; dsm. forestæppendum 93.1; asm. forestæppendne 51.18.

forewītegan wv. pres. p. (*praesagus*) dsf. forewitegendra 104.1.

forflēon sv. *fugere*, pres. p. nsm. forfleonde 103.13.

forgǣgednyss sf. *excessus*, dp. forgægednissū 65.1.

forgeearnung sf. *meritum*, dp. forgeearnungum 132.1.

forgifestre wf. *datrix*, ns. 49.6.

forgyfan sv. *concedere, conferre, dare, dimittere, donare, largiri, laxare, remittere, tribuere*, ind. pres. 3 sg. forgyfð 68.1; pret. 2 sg. forgeafe 17.4; forgæfe 32. 2; 3 sg. forgeaf 74.15; opt. pres. 2 sg. forgyfe 47.15; 71. 2; forgife 23.11; 3 sg. forgyfe 8.15; 68.9; 93.14; forgife 24. 7; 143.10; pret. 2 sg. forgeafe 33.2; imp. sg. forgyf 11.5; 12.12; 21.8; 25.9; 53.16; 62. 13; 63.5; 65.4; 93.9; 94.16; 108.13; 116.3; 134.16; 136. 16; 138.14; inf. 37.10; pres.

pres. p. nsm. forgyfende 34.13; 80.6; 139.14; pp. forgyfen 90. 14; 106.5; 125.13; asn. forgifen 76.7.

forgyfenyss sf. *indulgentia, remissio, venia*, ns. 94.12; forgifenysse 142.2; gs. forgyfenysse 62.9; as. forgyfenysse 47.13; 71.3; 126.2; 131.16; forgyfennysse 32.2; 105.3; 126. 7; forgyfenessa 144.8; forgifenysse 105.13; forgifenyssa 118.4.

forgyfu sf. *gratia*, ds. forgyfe 78.7.

forhabban wv. *abstinere*, pres. p. nsm. forhæbbende 65.19.

forhæfednyss sf. *abstinentia, parsimonia*, gs. forhæfednysse 64.2; 66.10; ds. forhæfednysse 64.6; as. forhæfednysse 9.15; forehæfednyssa 63.1.

forhēafod sn. *frons*, dp. forheafdū 32.15.

forhtigan wv. *pavere, pavescere*, ind. pres. 3 sg. forhtað 31.18; 142.6; 3 pl. forhtiað 94.16.

forlǣtan rv. *deserere, intermittere, linquere*, ind. pres. 3 sg. forlæt 6.12; inf. forlætan 56.7; pres. p. nsn. forlætende 142.7.

forlēosan sv. *perdere*, opt. pret. 3 sg. forlure 50.8; pp. asn. forloran 59.8; apm. forlorene 91.20.

forma adj. *primus*, dsmn. forman 4.1; 24.18.

forma cyðere sm. *protomartyr*, ns. forma cyðere 46.4.

forma ðrōwere sm. *protomartyr*, ns. forma ðrowære 47.4.

forscrǣncan wv. *elidere*, pp. nsn. forscrǣncte 25.15.

forscrincan sv. pp. (*peraridus*) asn. forscruncen 132.6.

forsēon sv. *despicere, respuere, spernere*, ind. pret. 3 sg. forseah 74.4; 3 pl. forsawan 132.7; pres. p. apm. forseonde 131.7; pp. dpnf. forsewenum 14.11; 130.4.

forspenning sf. *inlecebra* ns. 64.8.

forspillan wv. *perdere*, ind. pret. 3 sg. forspilde (?); dpm. forspilledū 42.17.

forswǣlan wv. *concremare, cremare*, imp. sg. forswæl 36.6; pp. npm. forswælede 5.8.

forswǣð sn. *vestigium*, ap. forswaðu 38.16.

forswelgan sv. *sorbere*, opt. pres. 3 sg. forswelge 127.8.

forsworcenlic adj. *obscurus*, gsn. forsworcenlices 24.10.

forsworcennyss sf. *obscurum*, ap. forsworcennyssa 23.15; 37.2.

forðæncan wv. *reputare*, nsm. forðæncende 138.8.

forðālūtan, sv. pp. (*cernuus*) npm. forðalotene 5.15.

forðām conj. *quia*, forðā 85.9.

forðāmðe conj. *quia*, forðāðe 68.2.

forðan conj. *quia*, 33.7.

forðātēon sv. *edere, prodere, producere*, ind. pret. 2 sg. forðatuge 72.14; inf. forðateon 28.7; pp. npn. forðatogen 25.7.

forðbringan wv. *proferre*, imp. sg. forðbring 76.19; pres. p. nsf. forðbringende 19.17; vsm. forðbringende 13.13; 15.9.

forðeldegan wv. *sufferre*, ind. pret. 3 sg. forðeldegode 134.10.

forðgewitan sv. *praeterire*, pp. apn. forðgewitene 119.9.

forðīadv.*unde*,forði56.10;137.9.

forðrǣstan wv. *conterere*, ind. pres. 2 sg. forðræstest 32.14.

forðstæppan sv.*procedere, prodire*, ind. pres. 3 forðsteppað 78.1; pret. 3 sg. forðstop 53.5; 112.6; opt. pres. 3 sg. forðstæppe 16.18; pres. p. nsmn. forðstæppende 36.1; 44.5.

forðstæpping sf. *processus*, ds. forðstæppinga 80.14.

fortredan sv. *calcare, conculcare*, ind. pret. 3 pl. fortrædan 132. 10; pres. p. nsm. fortredende 85.1.

forwyrd smnf. *interitus*, ns. 127. 8; ds. forwerde 34.10.

fōstorcild sn. *alumnus*, ap. fostercild 97.10.

fōstorfæder sm.*altor*, ns. fostorfæder 65.18.

fōt sm.*pes*, ds. fét 85.1; as. fot 70.5; ap. fét 86.2.

fōtcopsigan wv. *compedire*, pp. apm. fotcopsede 125.4.

fōtswæð sn. *vestigium*, ap. fotswaðu 33.10; 78.6; 114.9; 138. 12.

fōtwelm sm. *planta*, ap. fotwelmas 61.7.

fram prep. w. dat. *a, ab* (fortythree times).

fremigan wv. *prodesse*, opt. pres. 3 sg. fremige 18.11.

frēo adj. *liber*, npm. frige 59.10.

frēols sm. *festa*, as. freols 120. 12; 136.18.

frēols adj. *festivus, festus*, nsm. freols 117.5; asm. freols 139.3; npf. freols 141.8.

frēolstīd sf. *festivitas*, gs. freolstide 73.15.

frēond sm. *amicus*, ns. freond 66.7; ap. freond 139.9.

frōfer sm.*paraclitus, solamen*,ns. frofer 93.18; ds. frofer 5.19; 138.17; as. frofer 49.12.

Frōfergāst sm. *Paraclitus*, nvs. 92.5; 97.15; 145.12; ds. frofergaste46.18; 93.12; 115.18; 125. 9; 135.1; frofer ... 1.12.

fruma wm.*primordium*,ds. fruman 31.1.

fugel sm. *ales*, ns. 18.13; 51.6.

fūl adj.*foedus, lubricus, sordidus*, nsmf. ful 5.5; 26.13; gsn. fules 30.4; dsn.fulum 3.9; asm.fulne 15.19.

full adj. *plenus*, nsnf. 110.6; 112.5.

fullfremman wv. *perficere*, pp. nsmf. fullfremed 123.18; 125. 13; fulfremed 106.5; 113.16; 130.17; dsn. fulfremedū 60.14.

fullice adv. *plene*, comp. fullicor 106.5; 125.13.

fulluht snf.*baptisma*,gs.fulluhtes 18.15; as. fulluhta 32.1.

fulluhtere sm. *Baptista*, vs. ful-luhttera 118.5.

fultum sm. *adjutorium, auxilium*, ds. fultume 49.12; as. fultum 60.9.

furlang sn. *stadium*, ns. 120.19.

fyligan wv. *sequi*, ind. pret. 3 pl. feligdon 132.7; inf. fylgian 66.9; fyligan 138.12; pres. p. nsm. fyligende 133.8; npm. fyligende 80.13; feligende 43.10.

fȳr sn. *ignis*, ns. fyr 92.7; 96.12; 143.8; fér 94.1; ds. fyre 29.12; 130.7; fire 10.7; dp. fyrum 5.7; 10.13.

fyrdwīc sn. *castra*, np. fyrdwycu 73.7.

fȳren adj. *igneus*, nsf. fyrenne 1.4; dsn. fyrenum 66.4; dsf. ferenre 22.9.

fyrmest adj. *primus*, dsm. fyrmstū 45.4.

fyrwit sn. *ardor*, ns. fyrwet 14.15; ferwyt 10.8.

G

gaderigan wv. *colligere*, ind. pres. 3 sg. gaderað 6.13.

gælsa wm. *luxus*, ds. gælsan 29.14.

gær, see **gēar**.

gærstapa wm. *locusta*, dp. gær-stapum 103.19.

Galilēaland sn. *Galilea*, ds. Galilealande 85.17; 86.4.

gālnyss sf. *libido*, ns. galnyss 5.3.

gān anv. *pergere*, ind. pres. 2 sg. gæst 140.9; pret. 3 pl. eodon 85.19; 86.5.

gang sm. *gressus*, dp. gangū 38.13.

gāst sm. *flamen, pneuma, spira-men, spiritus*, nvs. gast 10.1; 72.8; 92.1; 93.18; 94.8; 99.10; 135.15; 139.19; 145.12; 146.11; gs. gastes 8.7; 15.14; 16.12; 26.16; 42.4; 49.5; 94.16; 124.2; 130.20; ds. gaste 1.12; 5.19; 12.4; 33.22; 35.15; 40.10; 43.8; 43.18; 46.1; 54.6; 61.5; 72.18; 75.16; 77.17; 83.13; 97.8; 108.14; 118.19; 120.9; 138.17; as. gast 3.14; 65.12; 93.5; 95.4; 110.7; 141.19; gp. gasta 119.6.

gāstlic adj. *spiritalis*, nsf. gastlic 92.8; asf. gastlice 66.12.

geāhnigan wv. *possidere*, ind. pres. 3 sg. geahnað 134.12; 3 pl. geahniað 130.6; imp. sg. geahna 86.16.

gealga wm. *patibulum*, ds. gealgan 78.4.

gēancyrr sm. *reditus*, ds. gēan-cyrre 57.11.

gēar sm. *annus*, gs. geares 93.17; gæres 39.14; gp. geara 48.13; dp. gearū 103.12.

gearcigan wv. *adhibere, exhibere, parare, praebere, praeparare, praestare*, ind. pres. 2 sg. gearcast 132.18; pret. 2 sg. gearcodest 108.7; 3 sg. gearcode 103.16; opt. pres. 2 sg. gearcige 71.3; 3 sg. gearcige 24.8; imp. sg. gearca 62.8; 72.1; 77.7; 77.8; gearce 53.12; 65.5; pres. p. vsm. gearcigende 13.15; 70.2.

gēarlic adj. *annuus*, asm. gear-licne 106.16; asn. gearlic 79.17; npf. gearlice 141.7; dpf. gearlic-um 65.7; apmf. gearlice 73.15; 138.5.

geat sn. *janua*, *porta*, nvs. 76. 13; 112.4; 142.11; ns. gead 142.10.

geatweard sm. *janitor*, ns. 105. 14.

gebēcnan wv. *prodere*, ind. pres. 2 sg. gebecnest 104.3.

geberan sv. *bajulare, gerere*, ind. pret. 3 sg. gebær 50.11; 75.2; 139.2.

gebiddan sv. *adorare, deprecari, exorare, orare, poscere,* ind. pres. 3 sg. gebitt 65.2; 108.9; 1 pl. gebiddað 133.3; 3 pl. gebiddað 74.17; pret. 2 sg. gebæde 46.8; 3 pl. gebædon 48.10; opt. pres. 3 sg. gebidde 2.16; imp. sg. gebide 110.11; gebida 111.4; ger. to gebiddenne 60.1; prep. dpm. gebiddendum 96.7.

gebīgan wv. *curvare, flectere, reflectere,* opt. pres. 3 sg. gebige 91.4; pp. gebiged 108.10; pl. gebigede 35.2; apf. gebigede 104.18.

gebindan sv. *ligare*, pp. npm. gebundne 32.4.

gebisnung sf. *documentum*, dp. gebisnungum 73.2; ap. gibis-nunga 72.15.

gebletsigan wv. *benedicere*, pp. vsn. gebletsod 110.10; vsm. gebletsoda 125.7.

geblissigan wv. *gaudere*, ind. pres. 3 sg. geblissað 51.7; opt. pres. 3 sg. geblissige 20.9.

gebrǣdan sv. pp. (*torridus*) asm. gebrædne 82.6.

gebringan wv. *perducere, trans-ferre,* ind. pres. 2 sg. gebringst 131.8; inf. 125.12; gebringe 106.4.

gebycgan wv. *mercari*, ind. pret. 2 sg. gebohtest 13.6.

gebyrdtīd sf. *natalis*, gs. gebyrd-tide 40.6; 41.2; 42.21.

gecēlan wv. *refrigerare*, pres. p. nsm. gecelende 3.7.

gecēosan sv. *eligere*, pp. vsn. gecoren 79.1,

gecīgan wv. *vocare, vocitare,* ind. pres. 3 sg. gecigeð 18.16; pp. gecigeð 13.17; 43.6; 142.9. See cion.

geclǣnsigan wv. *emundare, mundare,* ind. pres. 3 sg. geclænsað 25.10; imp. sg. geclænsa 20.4; 67.7.

gecneordnyss sf. *studium*, dp. gecneordnyssū 72.3.

gecwēme adj. *gratuitus, gratus,* asm. gecwemne 20.2; apf. ge-cweme 146.12; sup. npf. ge-cwemēstan 146.14; apf. ge-cwemestan 99.1.

gecyrran wv. *revertere*, pp. dpm. gecyrredum 62.8.

gecȳðan wv. *pronuntiare*, pres. p. nsf. gecyðende 61.12.

gedafenigan wv. *decere*, ind. pres. 3 sg. gedafenað 43.16; 90.4; 146.5.

gedafenlic adj. *congruus*, dsf. gedafenlicre 38.1.

gedēfe adj. *quietus*, nsm. gedefe 137.2; dsf. gedefre 26.6; asf. gedyfe 12.12; dpf. gedefum 4.

15; apf. gedefa 93.10; apm. gedefan 3.12.

gedẹrigan wv. *laedere*, inf. gederian 32.19.

gedrǣfan wv. *confundere*, opt. pret. 3 pl. gedræfdon 17.2.

gedrēfan wv. pp. (*turbidus*) vpf. gedrefeda 21.10.

gedrēfednyss sf. *turbo*, dp. gedrefednyssum 127.7.

gedrimor, see gedwimor.

gedrȳme adj. *melodus, canorus*, nsf. gedryme 2.14; dpf. gedrymum 115.15.

gedweld sn. *erratum, error*, ns. 17.12; ds. gedwelde 24.6; gp. gedweldra 6.11; dp. gedweldum 126.2; ap. gedwyld 114.7.

gedwimor sn. *phantasma*, ns. gedrimor 30.5; np. gedwymeru 11.15.

gedȳfe, see gedēfe.

geēacnigan wv. *concipere*, ind. pres. 2 sg. geeacnast 110.7; pret. 3 sg. geeacnode 50.16; 54. 10; 75.9; 140.2.

geēacnung sf. *crementum, partus*, ns. geeacnung 41.4; 43.16; as. geeacunnge 43.14; dp. geeacnungum 104.13.

geēadmēdan wv. *adorare*, ind. pret. 3 pl. geeadmettan 86.2.

geearnigan wv. *merere, mereri*, ind. pres. 1 pl. geearniað 56. 4; pret. 3 sg. geearnode 47.10; 54.11; 104.6; 139.1; 136.19; 1 pl. geearnodon 127.11; 128. 3; 3 pl. geearnedon 120.13; opt. pres. 1 pl. geearnian 8.2; 128.4.

geearnung sf. *meritum*, ds. geearnunge 129.3; np. geearnunga 118.3; dp. geearnungum 33.17; 47.7; 71.1; 103.10; 104.8; 104. 16; 129.5; 136.2; 137.11; ap. geearnunga 124.14.

geēcan wv. *apponere, augere*, imp. sg. geéc 66.11; geic 131.10; pres. p. nsm. geecende 22.10; pp. geiht 104.3.

geedcẹnnan wv. *creare, renasci*, pp. geedcenned 141.15; npm. geedcynnede 43.8.

geedlēanend sm. *remunerator*, ns. geedeanend 33.18.

geedstaðeligan wv. *reformare*, ind. pret. 2 sg. geedstawelodest 103.6.

geẹndeberdigan wv. *ordinare*, pres. p. nsm. geendeberdiende 28.6.

geẹndigan wv. *determinare, peragere*, pres. p. nsm. geendigende 11.4; pp. dsm. geendedum 2.9; dsf. geendodre 94.10.

geẹndung sf. *terminus*, ds. geendunge 11.10; as. geendunga 22. 16; dp. geendungum 60.15.

gef, see gyf.

gefaran sv. *petere*, ind. pret. 3 sg. gefor 48.15.

gefēa wmf. *gaudium*, ns. gefea 42.21; 88.9; 89.9; 91.9; 91.21; 112.12; gs. gefean 55.9; ds. gefean 73.18; 83.8; 86.7; 130. 22; as. gefean 66.12; 143.11; gp. gefeana 28.17; dp. gefeanum 122.2; 123.5; 124.4; 128. 11; 136.4; ap. gefean 53.8; 57.11; 65.10; 93.16; 108.12; 127.12; 132.1; 134.5; 138. 7; 143.4.

gefēgednyss sf. *compago*, ns. gefegednyss 5.6.

gefellan wv. *complere, implere, refercire, replere*, ind. pret. 2 sg. gefeldest 93.8; 3 sg. gefelde 96.14; gefylde 94.8; opt. pret. 3 pl. gefeldon 135.11; imp. sg. gefell 26.18; gefyll 92.3; pp. gefelled 20.9; 124.4; 130.22; nsn. gefylled 54.6; 112.5; npm. gefellede 96.15; npn. gefyllede 78.13; apm. gefellede 106.9.

gefēra wm. *socius*, np. geferan 132.2.

gefēran wv. *petere*, ind. pret. 3 sg. geferde 45.16.

gefern, see **gefyrn**.

gefērrǣden, see **gefȳrrǣden**.

gefrætwigan wv. *adornare, ornare, vestire*, ind. pres. 3 pl. gefrætewiað 104.15; opt. pres. 3 pl. gefrætewion 120.16; pres. p. nsm. gefrætewigende 135.7; vsm. gefrætwigende 2.2; pp. vsn. gefrætewod 78.18.

gefrēdan wv. *sentire*, opt. pres. 3 sg. gefrede 143.8.

gefremigan wv. *patrare, peragere*, ind. pret. 3 sg. gefremode 70.3; pp. pl. gefremode 94.9; apm. gefremedan 56.8.

gefultumigan wv. *adjuvare, favere, juvare*, opt. pres. 2 sg. gefultumige 2.11; imp. sg. gefultuma 55.1; 129.7; 138.2; pp. pl. gefultumode 137.11.

gefyllan, see **gefellan**.

gefyrn adv. *dudum, olim, quondam*, 36.2; 39.10; 93.7; 94.17; 97.5; 98.1; 109.11; gefern 54.5; 69.5; 96.9.

gefȳrrǣden sf. *collegium, consortium*, ds. gefyrrædene 46.10; 124.6; geferrædene 131.2.

gegaderigan wv. *cognoscere, colligere*, ind. pret. 3 pl. gegaderudon 38.14; pp. pl. gegæderode 97.1.

gegaderung sf. *concio*, ns. 117.3.

gegrētan wv. *salutare*, pres. p. nsm. gegretende 110.4.

gegrīpan sv. *arripere*, ind. pres. 3 sg. gegripð 51.15.

gehæftan wv. *captivare, retinere*, pp. nsn. gehæft 83.1; apm. gehæfta 142.6.

gehǣlan wv. *salvare, sanare*, ind. pret. 2 sg. gehældest 34.12; imp. sg. gehæl 111.22; 124.17; 127.4; pres. p. nsm. gehælende 52.13; pp. pl. gehælede 119.12.

gehālgigan wv. *consecrare, dedicare, dicare, sacrare, sancire*, ind. pret. 2 sg. gehalgodest 64.4; gehalgodes 68.6; 3 sg. gehalgode 52.6; 65.19; pres. p. nsm. gehalgiende 53.3; pp. nsn. gehalgod 141.9; asm. gehalgodne 141.10; asn. gehalgod 143.9.

gehālgigend sm. *dicator*, vs. gehalgigend 64.2.

gehātan rv. *jubere*, pp. nsf. gehaten 52.17.

gehealdan rv. *conservare, custodire, servare*, opt. pres. 3 sg. gehealde 9.4; 27.18; 3 pl. gehealdan 60.11; imp. sg. geheald 35.11; 112.15; 119.2; geheold 132.16; pp. gehealdan 85.4; dsf. gehealdenre 64.6.

gehęfegan wv. *gravare*, pp. nsn. gehefegod 14.1; pl. gehefegode 126.3; 137.7.

gehelpan sv. *subvenire*, ind. pres. 2 sg. gehelpst 36.3; imp. sg. gehylp 117.14.

gehęnde adj. *proximus, propinquus*, nsm. gehende 19.4; asn. gehende 18.14.

gehęnde adv. *prope*, gehende 38.4.

gehēran, see gehȳran.

gehęrigan wv. *laudare*, pp. geherod 15.6.

gehērsumigan wv. *obsequi, obtemperare*, opt. pres. 3 sg. gehersumige 20.7; pres. p. nsm. gehersumigeende 70.15.

gehīwigan wv. *formare, informare*, opt. pres. 3 sg. gehiwige 16.1; pp. nsm. gehiwod 111.6.

gehlēowan wv. *fovere*, pres. p. nsm. gehleowende 9.7.

gehorwigan wv. *sordidare*, pres. p. nsf. gehorwigende 5.3.

gehrępigan wv. *attingere*, pp. nsm. gehrepod 74.6.

gehwǣde adj. *parvus*, dsf. gehwǣdre 51.5.

gehwerfan wv. *redire*, ind. pres. 3 sg. gehwerð 7.3; gehwyrfð 21.15; 3 pl. gehwerfað 141.7; pret. 3 sg. gehwerfde 83.4; inf. 53.18.

gehwilc prn. *quisque*, apf. gehwilce 37.2.

gehwilcnyss sf. *qualitas*, ds. gehwilcnysse 36.14.

gehwyrfan, see gehwerfan.

gehylpan, see gehelpan.

gehȳran wv. *audire, exaudire*, opt. pres. 3 sg. gehere 4.9; imp. sg. gehyr 34.9; 41.1; 80. 11; 111.14; 144.3; 146.3; geher 13.19; 62.2; 111.3; pl. gehyrað 122.8; inf. gehȳran 111.18; pp. dsf. gehyrdre 36.7.

geīcan, see geēcan.

geīdligan wv. *evacuare*, pp. nsn. geidlod 106.6.

geinsegeligan wv. *signare*, pp. asn. geinsegelod 124.18.

gelǣccan wv. *rapere*, opt. pres. 3 pl. gelǣccon 25.8.

gelǣdan wv. *ducere*, ind. pret. 3 sg. gelǣdde 48.7; pp. nsm. gelǣdd 59.5.

gelǣngan wv. *pervocare*, pp. dpf. gelængdum 90.3.

gelǣstan wv. *persolvere, solvere*, ind. pret. 1 pl. gelæston 2.12; gelæstan 147.4; opt. pres. 1 pl. gelæstan 120.6.

gelaðung sf. *ecclesia*, gs. gelaðunge 99.5; 112.11; 129.1; 135.8; gelaðunga 6.15; ds. gelaðunge 64.9; gp. gelaðunga 123.12; 129.13.

gelēafa wm. *fides*, ns. geleafa 3.3; 3.7; 7.6; 16.7; 16.10; 16. 15; 17.13; 28.1; 72.2; 113. 16; 123.16; geleaf 130.15; gs. geleafan 32.16; 44.20; 70.2; 135.14; ds. geleafan 3.4; 59.1; 106.8; as. geleafan 52.11.

geleaffull adj. *fidelis*, dsn. geleaffullum 78.14; dsm. geleaffullan 16.6; gpm. geleaffulra 48.3; 90.9; dpm. geleaffullum 53.12; apm. geleaffulle 53.4.

gelēaflēas adj. *perfidus*, gsm. geleaflease 35.12; asf. geleaflease 120.3; npf. geleaflease 99.16; apf. geleafleasan 97.13.

gelēaflic adj. *fidelis*, dsn. geleaflice 70.4.

gelęcgan wv. *ponere*, pp. nsm. geléd 103.8.

gelēfan wv. *credere*, ind. pres. 1 pl. gelefað 31.20; 53.18; 98. 11; gelyfað 42.13; 59.2; 88.8; opt. pres. 1 pl. gelyfan 93.6; pres. p. nsf. gelefende 75.10; gpm. gelefendra 112.13; 120. 4; 123.17; 130.16; gelyfendra 34.7; dpm. gelefendum 18.10; apm. gelyfende 42.6; pp. gelyfed 12.7.

gelīc adj. *aequalis, par, similis*, nvsmf. gelie 44.13; 59.14; 34. 2; 73.2; asm. gelicne 31.4; 42.11; npm. gelice 38.13; 136. 3.

gelimp sn. *casus*, dp. gelimpum 17.11.

gelimplic adj. *aptus*, asf. gelimplice 19.17.

gelimplice adv. *apte*, 72.11.

gelīðewǣcan wv. *allevare, mitescere, reficere, relevare*, ind. pres. 3 pl. geliðewæcað 6.14; opt. pres. 2 sg. geliðewæce 6.4; 3 sg. geliðewæce 2.7; imp. sg. geliðewæc 129.4; pp. dpn. geliðewæhtum 14.10.

gelōgigan wv. *collocare, locare*, opt. pret. 1 p. gelogode 121.2; pp. gelogod 24.2.

gelōmlīce adv. *crebro*, gelomlice 116.7.

gelustfulligan wv. *oblectare*, pres. p. nsn. gelustfulligende 58.6.

gelўfan, see gelēfan.

gemaca wm. *compar*, vs. 5.18; 139.18.

gemængan wv. *miscere*, pres. p. nsm. gemængende 47.9.

gemǣnigfyldan wv. *cumulare*, pp. gemænigfyld 104.14.

gemǣnnyss sf. *contubernium*, as. gemænnysse 31.16.

gemǣre sn. *finis, limes, terminus*, ds. gemære 74.3; as. gemære 17.4; 50.2; dp. gemærum 99. 4; 120.4; ap. gemæru 35.8.

gemāh adj. *pervicax*, nsn. gemah 142.6.

gemeagan, see gemetegian.

gemedemigan wv. *dignari*, opt. pres. 3 sg. gemedemige 104. 22; imp. sg. gemedema 10.3; 111.18; pp. gemedemod 31. 12; 32.6; 32.18; 32.22.

gemęngednyss sf. *mixtum, confusum*, nvp. gemengednyssa 17. 2; 21.10.

gemētan wv. *invenire*, opt. pres. 3 sg. gemete 17.13.

gemetegian wv. *temperare*, ind. pres. 2 sg. gemetegast 10.11; opt. pres. 3 sg. gemetegie 3.8; 9.5; 17.7; pres. p. nsm. gemeagende 108.16.

gemiltsigan wv. *ignoscere, indulgere, miserari, propitiare,* opt. pres. 2 sg. gemiltsige 18.10; imp. sg. gemiltsa 20.16; 33.5; 33.6; 68.2; 91.14; 131.12; pp. nsm. gemiltsod 8.14; 46.11.

gemunan swv. *meminisse,* imp. 1 sg. gemun 13.7; 39.9.

gemundigan wv. *fovere,* imp. sg. gemunda 3.16.

genēolǣcan wv. *approximare,* opt. pres. 3 sg. geneolǣce 20.8.

genēosigan wv. *adire, appetere, petere, visere, visitare,* ind. pres. 2 sg. geneosast 73.6; 3 sg. geneoseð 97.16; pret. 3 sg. geneasude 45.15; opt. pres. 2 sg. geneosige 113.4; imp. sg. geneosa 92.2; inf. geneosigan 116.12; pres. p. apm. geneosigende 142.11.

genęrigan wv. *eripere, eruere,* ind. pret. 3 sg. generode 111.10; opt. pres. 3 sg. generige 59.11; imp. sg. genere 42.8; pres. p. nsm. generigende 19.14; pp. npm. generode 82.11.

genihtsum adj. *affluus, opimus, profluus,* dsn. genihtsumū 135.6; npm. genihtsume 94.3; dpf. genihtsumū 58.6; 104.16; apf. genihtsuma 113.11.

genihtsumlice adv. *affatim,* 5.2; 29.18; 58.8.

geniman sv. *assumere,* inf. 31.12.

genip sn. *nubes, nubilum,* ds. genipe 91.18; ap. genipu 74.2; vp. genipu 21.9.

genyrwigan wv. *artare,* pp. pl. genyrwode 36.13.

geoc sn. *jugum,* ds. geoce, 70.11.

geoffrigan wv. *immolare, offerre,* pp. geoffrod 78.8; 82.14; 82.16.

geolu adj. *fulvus,* dpm. geolowum 19.18.

gēomrigan wv. *gemere,* ind. pret. 3 sg. geomrode 31.10; pres. p. nsf. geomriende 84.17; npm. geomrigende 21.7; npm. geomriende 117.12.

gēomrung sf. *gemitus,* dp. geomrungum 85.7; ap. geomrunga 128.2.

geond prep. w. acc. *per,* 1.9; 3.15; 39.14; 47.2; 49.18; 55.13; 66.3; 68.12; 73.7; 75.4; 88.12; 104.4; 106.14; 112.7; 124.14; 133.6; 136.18; 137.12; 141.20; 145.7; geon. 39.8; geonde 137.12.

geondblāwan rv. *afflare,* pp. dsn. geondblawenū 96.16.

geondgēotan sv. *fundere, perfundere, refundere,* ind. pret. 2 sg. geondgute 105.11; pp. nsm. geondgoten 10.4; npm. geondgoten 75.5; apf. geondgeotene 62.5.

geondhwerfan wv. *reducere,* pres. p. nsm. geonhwerfende 58.6.

geondlēohtend sm. *perlustrator,* vs. geondleohtend 128.5.

geondscīnan sv. *perlustrare,* opt. pres. 3 sg. geondscine 113.16.

geondsęndan wv. *fundere,* pp. geondsænd 75.18.

geondstrēdan wv. *spargere,* ind. pres. 3 sg. geondstret 30.1; pp. asn. geondstred 27.12.

geopenigan wv. *aperire, reserare*, ind. pres. 2 sg. geopenast 106. 2; geopenas 124.12; pres. p. nsm. geopenigende 83.6.

geornfull adj. *intentus, jugis, sedulus*, nsmf. 19.7; 70.13; dsm. geornfullū 49.11; dsf. geornfulre 111.15.

georstenlic adj. *hesternus*, nsm. georstenlica 47.5.

gereccan wv. *referre, retexere*, ind. pres. 1 pl. gereccað 135.5; inf. gereccan 132.17.

gereord sn. *lingua*, dp. gereordum 94.5; 97.4.

gerihtlǣcan wv. *corrigere, dirigere*, opt. pres. 3. sg. gerihtlǣce 113.14; 114.9; 116.16; 3 pl. gerihtlǣcan 61.8; imp. sg. gerihtlǣc 7.8; 104.19.

gerȳne sn. *mysterium, sacramentum*, ap. gerynu 66.5; 68.8.

gerȳnelic adj. *mysticus*, ds. gerynelicum 43.18; npn. gerynelican 94.9.

gerȳuu sf. *mysterium, mysticus*, gs. geryne 113.1; ds. geryne 96. 2; as. geryne 42.12; gerynu 61. 1; np. geryne 78.2.

gesǣlig adj. *felix*, vsmn. gesælig 72.17; 76.13; 104.8; dsm. gesæligū 57.11.

gesǣliglice adv. *feliciter*, gesæliglice 117.8.

gescæft snf. *creatura, factura, plasma, res*, as. gescæft 53.7; 124.17; np. gescæfte 146.1; gp. gescæfta 6.1; 10.11; 11.1; 11. 11; 20.11; 23.5; 28.9; 30.14; 58.9; gesceaft 91.1.

gescildan wv. *protegere, tueri*, opt. pres. 3 sg. gescilde 13.1; 37.16; imp. sg. gescild 49.8; gescyld 136.15; inf. gescyldan 120.14; pp. npm. gescilde 82.9.

gescyppan sv. *condere, creare, plasmare*, ind. pret. 2 sg. gesceope 31.2; 31.14; 92.4; gescope 145.18; 3 sg. gescop 50. 8; 75.21; 111.5; pp. nsmf. gesceapen 4.2; 91.3.

gesęcgan wv. *dicere, ferre*, pp. gesæd 92.5; 142.3.

gesęllan wv. *dare*, pp. geseald 90.11; 136.9.

geseohð, see gesihð.

geséon sv. *cernere, videre*, ind. pres. 2 sg. gesihst 21.5; 33.10; 1 pl. geseoð 43.9; pret. 3 sg. geseah 66.6; ind. pret. 3 pl. gesawon 51.17; 86.10; 87.8; 88.2; opt. pres. 3 sg. geseo 129.2; imp. sg. geseoh 141.4; 141.5; pl. geseoð 128.2; ger. to geseonne 85.18; inf. geseon 54.15; 56.12; 86.5; pres. p. nsm. geseonde 7.8; npm. geseonde 77.9; 86.1; 91.5; pp. gesewen 74.11.

geséðan wv. *testari*, ind. pret. 3 sg. geseðde 49.4; pp. geseðed 39.13.

gesęttan wv. *conserere, constituere, statuere*, opt. pres. 3 sg. gesette 12.16; 114.14; pres. p. nsm. gesettende 22.12.

gesihð sf. *conspectus, visus*, ds. gesihðe 86.10; geseohðe 114. 17; as. gesihðe 9.7.

gesíða wm. *comes*, np. gesiðan 38.13.

geslēan sv. *caedere, percutere*, pp. nsf. geslægen 21.14; pl. geslægene 132.13.

gesmēðigan wv. *planare*, pres. p. nsm. gesmeðiende 104.18.

gestrangigan wv. *vegetare*, ind. pret. 3 sg. gestrangode 137.3.

gestrēonan wv. *lucrari;* inf. gestreonan 73.4; pp. pl. gestrinode 73.8.

gesundfulligan wv. *secundare*, opt. pres. 3 sg. gesundfullige 16.3; imp. sg. gesundfulla 79.18; pp. (*secundus*) nsm. gesundfullod 28.3.

gesundfulnyss sf. *prosperum*, np. gesundfulnyssa 116.8.

geswǣs adj. *blandus*, dsn. geswæsum 85.15.

geswǣsnyss sf. *blandimentum*, ap. geswæsnyssa 134.6.

geswīcan sv. *cedere*, ind. pret. 3 sg. geswac 132.11.

geswinc sn. *labor*, gs. geswinces 2.6.

geswuteligan wv. *monstrare*, ind. pres. 3 sg. geswutelað 48.6; 67.6; imp. sg. geswutela 77.3; pp. geswutelod 65.17.

getācnigan wv. *signare*, ind. pres. 3 sg. getacnað 96.4; pp. npm. getacnode 32.15.

getǣl sn. *numerus*, ds. getæle 60.14; 94.11.

getēon sv. *ducere, trahere*, pp. getogen 61.10; asm. getogenne 70.14.

geðæncan wv. *cogitare*, ind. pres. 3 sg. geðæncð 14.3.

geðafigan wv. *consentire, sinere*, opt. pres. 2 sg. geðafige 125.1; imp. sg. geðafa 3.5; pres. p. nsn. giðafi . . . 12.15.

geðeld sn. *patientia*, as. 132.16.

geðēodan wv. *conjungere, haerere, jungere*, ind. pret. 2 sg. geðeoddest 31.15; opt. pres. 2 sg. geðeode 124.7; 131.3; 3 sg. geðeode 46.14; inf. geðeodan 47.15; pp. geðeod 89.12; 111.21; pl. geðeodde 120.13.

geðēodnyss sf. *junctus*, as. geðeodnes 13.16.

getimbrung sf. *fabrica*, as. getimbrunge 91.11.

getīðigan wv. *annuere, praestare*, opt. pres. 2 sg. getiðige 143.2; 3 sg. getiðige 73.11; 117.4; getidie 8.5; 8.18; imp. sg. getiða 5.17; 10.18; 17.17; 49.11; 63.4; 65.11; 65.12; 66.13; 124.13; 138.11; gitiða 10.9; 11.9; 12.1; 14.9; 15.7.

getrīwe adj. *fidus*, apn. getriwa 96.13.

getrymman wv. *firmare*, pres. p. nsm. getrymmende 17.5; 44.16; 92.16.

getwifeldan wv. *duplicare*, pp. npm. getwifeld 104.13.

getwinne num. *bini, geminus*, gsf. getwinre 44.7; vpm. getwinne 106.7.

gewǣcan wv. pp. (*fessus, saucius*) nsm. gewæht 37.6; dpm. gewæhtum 58.5; 142.1; apn. gewæhte 2.7.

gewæmmednyss sf. *corruptio*, gs. gewæmmednyssa 140.16.

gewǽpnigan wv. *armare*, pp. nsf. gewæpnod 130.9.

geweldan rv. *domare, refrenare, satiare*, ind. pres. 2 sg. geweldest 84.12; pret. 3 sg. gewelde 139.7; inf. gewyldan 139.6; pres. p. nsm. geweldende 9.5.

gewelgian wv. *ditare, munerare*, ind. pres. 2 sg. gewelgas 92. 12; opt. pres. 3 sg. gewelgie 4.16; pp. (*praeditus*) vsm. gewelegod 91.10; pl. gewelegode 29.18; 133.2.

gewęmman wv. *maculare*, inf. gewēman 103.14.

geweorðan sv. *efficere, facere*, opt. 3 sg. gewurðe 56.16; pp. geworden 43.19; 50.14; 54. 7; 66.2; 76.4; 79.5; 94.12; 112.4; npm. gewordene 5. 14; 136.3.

gewilnigan wv. *ambire, desiderare, gestire*, ind. pret. 3 sg. gewilnode 139. 6; opt. pres. 3 sg. gewilnige 14.15; pp. nsm. gewilnod 75.17; asf. gewilnode 86.6.

gewilnung sf. *desiderium, volum*, vs. 83.17; dp. gewilnungum 2. 11; 15.16; 54.17; 89.1; 114. 18; 122.7.

gewinn sn. *bellum, proelium*, gs. gewinnes 89.5; 123.13; 129. 14; ds. gewinne 42.7.

gewīscan wv. *optare*, pp. nsm. gewiscod 89.1; asm. gewiscodne 54.15.

gewiss adj. *certus*, apn. gewisse 35.8.

gewissigan wv. *regere*, ind. pres. 2 sg. gewissast 6.2; 26.2; 91. 11; opt. pres. 3 sg. gewissige 16.5; pres. p. asm. gewissigendue 75.1.

gewisslice adv. *certe*, 68.4.

gewita wm. *testis*, ns. 33.7.

gewītan sv. *exire, transire*, opt. pres. 3 sg. gewite 16.13; pres. p. vsn. gewitende 36.2.

gewītendlic adj. *caducus*, apmn. gewitendlice 134.7; 138.8.

gewitlēas adj. *insanus, vesanus*, gsm. gewitleases 130.10; dsm. gewitleasum 97.8.

gewitlēast sf. *vecordia*, ns. gewitleast 9.10.

gewītnigan wv. *punire*, opt. pres. 3 sg. gewitnige 37.15.

gewittig adj. *conscius*, nsn. 132. 15.

gewittnyss sf. *testimonium*, ds. gewittnysse 97.14.

gewlitigan wv. *decorare*, pres. p. nsn. gewlitigende 105.12.

gewrit sn. *scriptum*, dp. gewritum 73.8.

gewrīðan sv. *astringere, illigare, religare*, ind. pres. 3 sg. gewrið 14.4; opt. pres. 3 sg. gewriðe 15.19; imp. sg. gewrið 29.2.

gewrixl sn. *vicis*, as. 36.11; 91. 6; ap. 10.11.

gewuldorbēagigan wv. *coronare, decorare*, ind. pres. 3 pl. gewuldorbeagið 104.12; pp. (*laureatus*) nsm. gewuldorbeagod 47. 8; npm. gewuldorbeagode 105. 17.

gewuna wm. *usus,* ds. gewunan 2.6.

gewundigan wv. *vulnerare,* pp. gewundod 78.9.

gewunelic adj. *solitus,* dsf. gewunelicre 11.12.

gewurðigan wv. *colere,* pp. gewurðod 47.4; 117.5.

gewyldan, see geweldan.

geyppan wv. *depromere, edere, pandere, pangere, prodere, promere,* ind. pres. 1 pl. geyppað 21.6; 58.9; 131.11; 132.2; 146.13; pret. 3 sg. geypte 103. 3; 103.11; imp. pl. geyppað 57.1; 57.4; 57.7; 57.17; 58. 4; inf. 132.3; pp. asm. geyppodne 61.4.

gibīsnung, see gebīsnung.

giddigan wv. *canere,* ind. pret. 3 sg. gyddode 54.6; 3 pl. giddodan 103.20.

gīfernyss sf. *gastrimargia,* gs. giuernysse 64.7.

gifu, see gyfu.

gilt, see gylt.

giðafigan, see geðafigan.

gitīðigan, see getīðigan.

glæd adj. *alacris, placatus, placidus,* nsm. 44.8; 99.2; 113.4; 119.4; npf. glæde 143.6.

glædlice adv. *alacriter,* 120.6.

glęnga wm. *pompa,* ds. glengan 85.5.

glitinigan wv. *rutilare,* ind. pres. 3 sg. glitenað 47.3; 84.14; pres. p. nsm. glitinigende 8.11.

gnornung sf. *maeror,* ns. 142.3.

God sm. *Deus, numen,* nvs. (thirty-six times); gs. godes (twenty-four times); ds. gode (thirty times); as. (nine times).

gōd adj. *bonus,* nsm. god 33.14; vsm. gode 105.18; 124.9; 125. 6; 132.8; dpnf. godum 20.9; 36.12; 136.2; apn. godu 77.2.

godcundnyss sf. *deitas, divinitas,* ns. godcundnes 8.5; gs. godcundnysse 42.3; ds. godcundnysse 68.10; 145.6; vs. godcundnys 145.15; godcundnyss 34.2; 59.14; 133.3.

godewębb sn. *purpura,* ds. godewebbe 78.18.

gōdnyss sf. *bonitas,* vs. godnyss 145.15.

grama wm. *ira,* as. graman 71.2.

Grēcisc adj. *Graecus,* npm. grecisces 97.2.

grēnnyss sf. *viror,* ds. grénnysse 20.4.

gung adj. *lener,* dp. gungum 103. 12.

gūðfana wm. *labarum, vexillum,* as. guðfana 32.16; 80.16; np. guðfanan 44.3; 78.1.

gyddigan, see giddigan.

gyf conj. *si,* 68.1; 68.3; gef 7.9.

gyfu sf. *charisma, gratia, munus,* ns. gyfe 50.10; gs. gyfe 15. 18; 17.10; 49.6; 90.11; 92.9; gife 20.4; ds. gyfe 2.4; 65.4; 70.2; 91.16; 92.3; 93.8; 110. 6; 112.5; 127.5; gyfa 75.5; as. gyfe 16.4; 59.3; 62.9; 71.3; gife 23.11; np. gife 130.14; gp. gyfa 28.18; ap. gyfa 134.12.

gylt sm. *culpa, debitum, delictum*, ns. 3.6; 7.10; 15.1; 23.14; 25.13; gs. gyltes 23.3; ds. gylte 30.8; as. 6.16; 37.10; 53.15; gilt 15.19; dp. gyltum 14.4; 77.13; 91.14; 97.18; 139.14; ap. gyltas 133.4; 141.14.

gyrdel sm. *strophium*, as. 103.17.

gyrla wm. *stola*, dp. gyrlum 82.2.

H

habban anv. *habere*, ind. pres. 3 sg. habbað 61.7; inf. 52.12; negative : ind. pres. 3 sg. næfð 109.7.

hād sm. *sexus*, as. had 139.7.

hādelice adv. *personaliter*, hadelice 29.6.

hæftling sm. *captivus*, ap. bæftlingas 84.6; 125.3.

hæl sf. *salus, sanitas*, ns. hæl 7.4; 39.16; 42.5; 55.5; 105.6; 122.14; 136.9; 137.13; 142.1; 145.16; gs. hæle 32.8; 39.9; 61.4; 79.15; 80.4; 89.14; 110.2; 114.5; 116.13; ds. hæle 64.4; 137.6; as. hæle 8.15; 10.16; 117.16.

hælan wv. *curare, sanare*, opt. pres. 2 sg. hæle 32.20; 116.15; imp. pl. hælað 123.1.

Hælend sm. *Jesus, Salor*, nvs. hælend 7.7; 48.1; 64.1; 83.16; 87.11; 87.12; 104.20; 117.8; 117.13; 125.7; 137.17; 140.1; 145.11; gs. hælendes 87.8; 126.9; ds. hælende 90.14; as. hælend ˙12.2; 19.5; 77.9; 88.4; 127.6.

hǣs sf. *jussum*, ds. hæse 122.12; dp. hæsum 20.7.

hǣte wf. *calor, vapor*, ds. hætan 16.7; 96.14; as. bætan 3.8; 10.15.

hǣðen adj. *barbarus, gentilis*, gsf. hæðenre 98.16; npm. hæðen 97.2; gpm. hæðenra 94.6.

hāl adj. *salvus*, npm. hale 43.11; see **hāl** sȳ ðū.

hālig adj. *almus, sacer, sacratus, sacrosanctus, sanctus*, nvs. balig 27.14; 38.5; 47.3; 73.3; 76.11; 89.2; 96.12; 104.15; 118.9; 130.12; 136.17; 138.4; 145.12; 145.14; 146.11; nvsm. halga 12.9; 33.19; 34.6; 35.9; 46.3; 72.7; 72.14; 72.17; 73.5; 73.10; 73.13; 102.4; 129.5; 139.13; 139.19; 141.1; gsmn. haliges 11.7; 49.5; 130.5; 133.16; 138.3; gsf. haligre 49.6; 129.2; gsm. halgan 8.6; 15.14; dsmn. halgum 40.4; 45.8; 46.1; 74.6; 75.22; 94.11; 96.16; 108.14; 124.18; dsf. haligre 76.2; 137.5; ds. halgan 1.1; 12.4; 33.22; 35.15; 40.10; 42.4; 43.8; 54.5; 62.4; 75.16; 77.17; 83.13; 105.13; 118.19. 120.9; 121.4; 125.9; 135.1; dsm. hangan 60.4; asm. haligne 58.1; 82.5; 95.4; 139.15; halgan 65.12; 141.18; asf. halige 61.1; vsmf. halige 10.1; 14.17; 20.15; 62.6; 80.10; 127.5; 145.10; npmf. halige 42.13; 122.4; 141.13; gpm. halgena 69.1; 116.1; 117.6; 120.12; 123.16; 126.1; 130.15; 132.1; 135.7; gpn. haligra 119.17; dp. halgum 8.2; 103.

17; 108.7; 113.5; 119.4; 120.
1; 128.12; 129.4; apmn. halige
79.2; 93.7; 104.22; 131.11;
apn. balig 96.9; 97.5; 98.1;
apnf. halgan 114.12; 128.6;
comp. nsm. haligre 104.5; sup.
dsf. halgestan 4.13; asf. halgast-
an 110.4; vsm. haligesta 22.7.

hālignyss sf. *sanctitas*, ds. halig-
nysse 111.2.

halsigan wv. *deprecari, supplicare*, imp. sg. halsa 129.3; ger.
to halsigenne 60.2; pres. p.
npm. halsigende 113.3; dpm.
halsigendum 147.2.

halsung sf. *supplicatio*, ns. 19.7.

hāl sȳ ðū interj. *ave, salve*, hal sy
ðu 76.10; 76.14; 79.11 (2);
98.3; 110.5; 146.8; 146.9.

hālwęnde adj. *salubris*, sup. npf.
halwendestan 146.15.

hana wm. *gallus*, ns. 6.18; ds.
hanan 7.3.

hand sf. *manus*, ns. 24.12; 130.
10; ap. handa 21.1; 78.6; 98.
13.

handgewrit sn. *chirographum*,
ds. handgewrite 59.12.

handhwīl sf. *momentum*, dp. hand-
wilum 145.3.

hangigan wv. *pendere*, ind. pret.
3 sg. hangode 79.4; 3 pl.
hangoden 130.11.

hātan rv. *jubere*, ind. pres. 2 sg.
hætst 28.7; opt. pres. 3 sg.
hate 60.3.

hē pers. prn. *hic, ille, ipse,
is, se, sese, suus*, nsm. he (107
times); nsf. heo 9.8; 20.2; 37.2;

37.3; 50.12; 50.16; 54.10 (2);
54.11; 75.10; 112.7; 132.7;
139.2; 139.6; 139.11; nsn.
hit (twenty-nine times); gsm.
his (nineteen times); hys 8.2;
38.15; 60.4; dsm. him 12.15;
24.8; 47.7; 73.12; 137.13; asm.
hine 32.17; 48.18; 86.1; 111.
12; hyne 52.12; him 132.6;
asn. hit 14.4; 24.2; 28.15; 28.
16; np. hi (thirty-three times);
npm. by 9.16; he 38.14; np. heo
5.14; 85.19; 86.2; 96.18; 109.
12; 120.17; 132.7; 136.4; 137.
8; 140.13; gpm. heora 65.1;
73.4; 124.6; 136.2; 136.14;
hera 85.12; dpm. heom 40.1;
117.11.

hēafod sn. *caput*, gs. heafedes
58.2.

hēah adj. *altissimus, altus, celsus,
coaltissimus*, gsm. bean 27.5;
dsm. hean 102.5; apn. hege
38.3; sup. gsm. hehstan 92.6;
dsm. hehstan 46.16; vsm. hehsta
90.8.

hēahęngel sm. *archangelus*, ns.
heahengel 110.1; vs. heahængel
113.2.

hēahfæder sm. *patriarcha*, gp.
heahfædera 118.2.

hēahnyss sf. *altum, arx, arduum,
altissimum, cacumen, culmen*, ds.
heahnysse 55.6; 88.4; 105.7;
114.11; 116.10; 137.14; as.
heahnyssa 70.6; dp. heanyssum
60.8; ap. heahnyssa 88.3.

healdan rv. *continere, custodire,
observare, reniti, retinere, tenere,*
pres. p. nsmf. healdende 35.5;
35.6; 35.8; 55.2; 75.13; 132.5;
npm. healdende 61.2.

hēalic adj. *altus, celsus, excelsus,*

eximius, sublimis, summus,
nvs. healic 53.5; 75.20; 76.5;
77.16; 104.8; 108.3; nsf. healice
57.8; 68.9; gsm. healices 49.4;
healican 55.2; gsf. healicra 29.
3; lsm. healican 141.17; 142.
17; 143.13; dsf. healicre 47.6.
143.3; 145.6; healicra 55.6;
105.7; asm. healicne 90.2; vsm.
healica 67.1; apf. healice 88.3.

hēalice adv. praecipue, sup. hea-
licost 115.5; 129.5.

hēalicnyss sf. sublimitas, ns.
healicnyss 74.13.

heall sf. aula, ns. 44.6; heal
142.9; gs. healle 123.14; 126.
5; 130.1; ds. healle 112.9; 116.
6; 141.6; as. bealle 8.2.

heanon, see heonon.

hēap sm. caterva, cuneus, lurma,
ns. heap 52.3; np. heapas 118.
2; ap. heapas 18.6; 103.13.

heard adj. dirus, durus, dsn.
heardan 78.10; apm. hearde
104.17; sup. dsm. heardestan
82.11.

hęfe sm. moles, ap. hefas 23.4.

hęfelice adv. grave, graviter, hefe-
lice 67.6; hefylice 124.15.

hęfig adj. gravis, nsm. hefi 12.13.

hęfigtēmnyss sf. molestia, molestum, np. hefigtemnyssa 143.5;
dp. hefigtemnyssum 19.15.

hęll sf. Avernus, barathrum, inferi, infernus, Tartara, Tartarus,
ns. hell 84.17; 142.16; gs. belle
84.5; 85.8; hylle 5.7; ds. helle
44.11; 49.13; 79.6; 83.4; as.
belle 85.1; 128.3; np. helle 82.
18.

hęllic adj. infernus, gpn. hellicra
91.3.

hęllware smpl. inferi, dp. hell-
warū 32.21.

help sm. suffragium, np. helpas
118.13; dp. helpum 129.7; ap.
helpas 136.8.

helpan sv. adjuvare, imp. sg.
help 112.16.

hēofigan wv. lugere, vpt. pres. 1
pl. heofigan 56.9.

heofon swm. caelum, polus, ns.
21.11; 39.17; 84.15; 122.1;
124.4; 130.22; gs. heofones 2.
2; 8.3; 17.1; 22.7; 22.8; 27.3;
46.14; 54.9; 55.6; 75.5; 75.15;
76.4; 76.13; 90.2; 105.14;
111.1; 115.4; 121.2; 127.1;
136.20; 137.14; 139.12; he-
ofenes 38.12; heofonas 105.7;
as. heofon 30.1; 122.9; heofan
6.10; gp. heofona 4.12; 8.17;
14.5; 70.11; 88.3; 128.4; heof-
ena 62.6; hefona 60.7; dp.
heofonum 25.6; 49.3; 116.14;
ap. heofenas 45.16.

heofonbigende ptc. caelebs, npm.
heofanbiggende 5.14; heofonbigende 86.16.

heofoncęnned ptc. caeligenus,
apm. heofancennede 108.4.

heofone wf. caelum, polus, gs.
heofonan 142.10; ds. heofonan
17.4; 49.14; 53.5; 106.4; 125.
12; 127.3; as heofonan 106.2;
124.12; ap. heofonan 89.4; 90.
6; 105.12; 110.10.

heofonlic adj. caelebs, caelestis,
caelicus, supernus, nsf. 50.10;
nsn. heofonlice 52.8; gsn.
heofonlices 103.4; 115.6; gsf.
heofonlican 123.14; 126.5;
heofonlice 130.1; dsf. heof-

onlicre 91.16; 92.3; asn. heofonlic 72.14; vsm. heofonlica
72.6; heofonlice 132.8; npmn.
heofonlice 35.3; 105.1; 118.14;
gpmn. heofonlicra 51.7; 91.2;
113.2; 119.6; dpmn. heofonlic-
um 17.5; 55.11; 112.2; 117.
7; 119.16; 133.10; 138.9; dpn.
heofonlicon 131.8; 134.8; dpm.
heofonlican 47.15; apmn. heofonlice 51.16; 120.18; 127.10;
127.12.

heofonlice adv. *caelitus*, 26.11;
65.17; 90.14; 94.15; 116.6;
132.8.

hēofung sf. *luctus*, ap. heofunga
2.8.

heonon adv. *hinc*, 57.5; 66.5; 91.
13; 103.10; 108.8; 116.17;
heanon 80.5.

heononforð adv. *ex tunc*, heanon-
forð 106.14.

heorde, see **hyrde**.

heordrǣden, see **hyrdrǣden**.

heorte wf. *cor*, ns. 12.18; gs. heortan 2.13; 3.10; 9.9; 72.11;
ds. heortan 29.9; 68.3; 75.10;
104.1; 115.12; 132.15; 135.
17; as. heorte 19.8; 23.1; gp.
heortena 10.17; 23.8; 26.14;
114.16; 122.7; dp. heortum
1.5; 92.14; ap. heortan 86.16;
91.15.

hēow, see **hīw**.

hēr adv. *hic*, her 114.3; 114.4;
114.5; 134.5; 142.1; 142.5.

heretoga wm. *dux*, gs. heretogan
42.18; vp. heretogan, 129.14;
herelogan 123.13.

herigan wv. *canere, laudare*, ind.

pres. 3 sg. hyrað 40.3; 1 pl.
heriað 146.16; heryað 144.6;
opt. pres. 3 pl. herigan 1.6; 1.
9; 146.1; inf. herigan 50.3;
pres. p. npm. herigende 56.10;
gpm. herigendra 15.5.

herigendlic adj. *laudabilis, laudandus*, nsm. 60.5; vsf. heri-
gendlice 144.1.

hērðurh adv. *hic*, herðurh 141.
13.

herung sf. *drama, favor, laus*,
as. herunge 71.2; gp. herunga
26.3; 48.4; dp. herungū 84.15.

hidor adv. *huc*, 64.8.

hiht sm. *spes*, nvs. 27.4; 28.3;
39.6; 67.2; 89.3; 99.8; 112.
13; 123.17; 130.16; 145.17;
ds. hihte 59.2; hyhte 106.8.

hinderscipe sm. *nequitia*, as.
135.13.

hingrigan wv. *esurire*, ind. pres.
3 sg. hingrað 51.6.

hīw sn. *figura, forma*, ds. heowe
92.9; as. 31.11; 39.12; 53.6;
94.2; vs. 69.2.

bladan sv. *haurire*, opt. pres. 3
sg. hlade 9.8.

hladung sf. *haustus*, dp. hla-
dungum 58.6.

hlǣfdige sf. *domina*, ns. hlæfdige
108.6.

hlēoðrigan wv. *canere, concinere,
concrepare, praecinere*, ind. pres.
3 sg. hleoðrað 30.12; pret. 3
sg. hleoðrode 78.13; opt. pres.
3 sg. hleoðrige 14.14; 3 pl.
hleoðrion 2.13; pres. p. nsm.
hleoðrigende 18.12; 29.16;
npm. hleoðriende 115.1.

hlot sn. *sors*,nvs. 9.14; 134.2; ds. hlote 128.10; 139.6.

hlynigan wv. *excubare*, pres. p. npm. hlyniende 26.4.

hlynnan wv. *reboare*, ind. pres. 3 sg. hlynð 8.7.

hōc sm. *ungula*, ns. hoc 132.11.

hogigan wv. *satagere*, imp. sg. hoga 106.4; 125.12.

hogung sf. *nisus*, dp. hogungū 8.12.

hopa wm. *spes*, ns. 7.3; 98.7.

hoppetan wv. *gestire*, pres. p. nsm. hoppetende 51.1.

borh sn. *luvio, sordes*, ds. horuwe 37.6; 104.21; dp. horwum 4. 11; 29.9; ap. horu 23.2; 23.10.

horig adj. *sordidus*, nsm. 26.13.

hræd adj. *promptus*, nsm. 10.3.

hrædlice adv. *concite, ociter, prompte, quantocius, strenue*, 6. 17; 85.19; 103.5; comp. hrædlicor 4.6; 85.18; 142.8.

hrēaw smn. *funus*, ds. hwreawe 85.6.

hrēosan sv. *corruere, ruere, sub-ruere*, opt. pres. 3 sg. hreose 25.16; hreosa 30.6; 1 pl. hreosan 27.2.

hreppan wv. *tangere*, inf. 79.2.

hrepung sf. *contactus*, ds. brepunga 42.19.

hrif, see rif.

hundfeald adj. *centeni*, dsmn. hundfealdū 104.14; dsf. hundfealdra 73.5.

hunig sn. *mel*, dp. hunigum 103. 19.

hunigswēte adj. *mellifluus*, apf. hunigswete 98.10.

hunigtēar sm. *nectar*, gs. hunigteare 79.8.

hūruðinga adv. *saltem*, huruðinga 103.14.

hūs sn. *domus*, ns. 50.13; 141. 9; ds. huse 54.14; 55.13.

hūð, see ūð.

hwā indef. prn. *quis*, nsm. hwa 68.1; see swā hwā, and swā hwā swā.

hweogul sn. *rota*, as. 22.12.

hwēollāst sm. *orbita*, ns. hweollāst 93.17.

hwilc int. prn. *quis*, nsf. 84.1; 132.17; see swā hwilc.

hwīt adj. *albus*, dpm. hwitum 82.2.

hwītigan wv. *albescere*, ind. pres. 3 sg. hwitað 21.11.

hwu adv. *quam*, 108.1.

hyll, see hell.

hȳnð sf. *suspendium*, ap. hynðe 59.7.

hyrde sm. *custos, pastor*, nvs. 51.10; 124.9; ds. 115.9; as. 42.16; vs. heorde 98.15; 105. 18; dp. hyrdum 51.9.

hyrdrǣden sf. *custodia*, ds. heordrædene 11.13; as. hyrdrædene 65.6.

hyrigan, see herigan.

hyseberðor sn. *puerpera*, ds. hyseberðre 50.17.

I

ic pers. prn. *ego*, ns. 19.4; np. we (156 times); gp. ure 13.7; 120.15; dp. us (fifty-one times); ap. us (sixty-three times).

ic ðe rel. prn. *qui, quique*, np. we ðe 4.13; 29.15; 40.4; 124. 15; 128.3.

īdelgelp sn. *jacentia, jactantia*, ns. idelgelp 25.14; 126.11.

īdelnyss sf. *vanitas, vanum*, ap. idelnysse 9.8; ydelnysse 17.15.

ilca prn. *idem*, asn. ilce 73.11; ylce 15.3.

inbringan wv. *inferre*, ind. pret. 3 sg. inbrohte 15.1.

incund adj. *intimus*, nsf. incunde 98.8; asn. incunde 14.5.

incundnyss sf. *intimum*, np. incundnes 9.9.

infæreld sn. *aditus, porta*, ns. infereld 76.6; as. infæreld 128. 4.

infaran sv. *intrare*, ind. pres. 3 sg. infærð 21.11; opt. pres. 3 pl. infaran 76.3.

inferan wv. *intrare*, ind. pret. 3 sg. inferde 50.10.

ingān anv. *ingredi*, inf. ingan 8.3; ger. in to ganne 61.17.

ingang sm. *aditus*, as. 61.17.

ingehȳd sfn. *conscientia*, ns. ingehyd 67.5; gs. ingehyde 33. 9; ingehedes 32.4; ap. ingehyd 127.4.

inlęnda wm. *accola*, ap. inlendan 57.5.

inlic adj. *intimus*, nsm. inlica 66.7.

innoð sm. *penetrale, venter, viscus*, gs. innoðes 43.20; ds. innoðe 111.8; np. innoðas 75.6; 96. 15; 130.11; dp. innoðum 108. 7; ap. innoðas 50.9; 78.5; 132. 12.

intinga wm. *gratia*, ds. intingan 80.4.

īsen adj. *ferreus*, apf. isene 99.3.

J

Jūda wm. *Juda*, ds. judan 42.16.

Jūdēisc adj. *Judaeus*, nsf. judeisc 97.7.

K

kyng, see cyng.

kȳðan, see cȳðan.

L

lā interj. la 132.17.

lāc sfn. *munus*, gs. lace 43.9; 92.9; ds. lace 14.2; 15.2; 52.2; 75.11; 95.3; 133.11; as. lac 48. 12; nvp. lac 63.7; 123.8; 129. 9; ap. lac 28.18; 33.2; 132.18.

lāce sm. *medicus*, ns. læce 33. 14; as. læce 116.13.

lǣcedōm sm. *medela, medicina, remedium*, ns. læcedom 142.1; as. læcedom 26.8; 34.13; 53. 16; 62.13.

lǣran wv. *docere*, ind. pret. 3 sg. lærde 97.12.

lamb sn. *agnus*, ns. 37.9; 52.8; 82.14; gs. lambes 82.1.

lange adv. *diu*, 24.5.

langsum adj. *longus*, dsn. langsumū 143.11.

lār sf. *doctrina, dogma*, gs. lare 72.15; ap. lara 38.14.

lārēow sm. *doctor, magister*, nvs. lareow 72.13; 105.14; 106.3; 125.11; 129.6; gs. lareowes 61.3; 120.19; gp. larewa 113. 10.

lāðlic adj. *horridus*, asn. ladlic 30.7.

lāttēow sm. *ductor, dux*, ds. latteowe 93.1; vs. latteow 98.6.

leaht, see **leoht**.

leahtor sm. *crimen, vitium*, gs. leahtres 26.15; 36.14; 118.8; 134.4; 138.14; ds. leahtre 14. 1; 78.11; np. leahtras 23.12; gp. leahtra 23.4; 25.11; 63.3; 99.2; dp. leahtrum 20.16; 72. 2; ap. leahtras 56.9; 65.3; 84. 2; 112.15; 128.7; 131.15; leahtres 139.14.

leahtrigan wv. *culpare*, ind. pres. 3 sg. leahtrað 91.7.

lēas adj. *mendax*, nsf. leas 24.12.

lēasung sf. *falsum, falsus*, np. leasinga 17.16; ap. leasunga 97.13.

lęnden sn. *lumbus*, ap. lendenu 29.11.

lēo wm. *leo*, gp. leona 66.6.

lēof adj. *carus*, nsm. leof 66.1; apf. leofa 124.14.

lēogan sv. *fallere*, inf. leogan 33. 8.

lēoht sn. *lumen, lux*, nvs. leoht 6.7; 7.11; 12.5; 12.7; 15.10; 18.2; 21.11; 22.5; 24.3; 27. 14; 34.7; 39.5; 69.2; 98.5; 99.10; 105.11; 136.11; 142. 2; 145.16; gs. leohtes 8.11; 9. 1; 11.3; 11.10; 12.7; 13.12; 13.14; 15.2; 15.10 (2); 17. 14; 18.1; 18.2; 22.15; 30.3; 57.5; 76.6; 84.14; 105.11; 108.12; 108.13; 114.11; 128. 11; ds. leohte 2.3; 14.18; 15. 9; 22.4; 22.10; 24.2; 24.18; 26.18; 30.11; 52.1; 94.1; 96. 11; 96.16; 105.10; 108.1; 120.16; 124.18; as. leoht 1.5; 12.8; 13.13; 15.9; 17.13; 18. 14; 19.12; 24.7; 27.12; 42.17; 43.9; 44.18; 52.1; 53.12; 76. 19; 92.13; nvp. leohta 105.15; 122.6; 123.15; vp. leoht 130.2.

leoht adj. *levis*, dsf. leahtre 103. 14.

lēohtfæt sn. *lampas, luminare*, gs. leohtfætes 127.9; vp. leohtfatu 126.5.

lēoma wm. *jubar, radius, spiculum*, nvs. leoma 15.14; 17.14; 30.3; 74.10; ds. leoman 21.14; 86.8; as. leoman 104.1; 127.2.

leornigan wv. *discere*, pres. p. nsm. leornigende 69.7.

leorningcniht sm. *discipulus*, np. leorningcnihtas 86.3; dp. leorningcnihtum 93.19.

lēoð sn. *carmen*, ns. leoð 55.8; ds. leoðe 78.14; np. leoð 1.6; dp. leoðum 58.9; ap. leoð 114. 12.

libban wv. *vivere*, ind. pres. 3 sg.
leofað 108.15; 1 pl. libbað 59.
1; 82.8; 111.12; inf. 86.1;
90.5; 106.10; pres. p. (*vividus*)
apn. libbende 28.10.

lic sn. *cadaver*, ap. licu 52.14.

liegan sv. *jacere*, ind. pret. 3 sg.
læg 111.8; inf. 51.3; pres. p.
apm. licgenda 6.18.

lichamlic adj. *corporeus*, dsf.
lichamlicre 86.10.

lichoma wm. *caro*, *corpus*, ns.
lichoma 26.13; 50.7; 62.14;
gs. lichoman 5.6; 31.11; 39.
10; 44.14; 44.15; 70.7; 79.
5; 89.8; 92.15; 106.10;
130.4; 133.16; 139.7; lichaman 139.4; ds. lichoman 13.
8; 16.6; 42.10; 42.15; 60.4;
86.12; 108.8; 115.12; lichaman 139.8; as. lichoman 24.
14; 50.6; 50.7; 82.5; lichoma
90.1; 141.11; np. lichoman 11.
17; gp. lichomena 10.16; 28.9;
ap. lichaman 52.13; 142.7.

lif sn. *vita*, nvs. lif 11.6; 69.
2; 79.13; 114.16; 136.10; 137.
3; gs. lifes 5.11; 14.2; 33.2;
53.8; 72.9; 83.2; 103.2; 105.
17; 114.14; 118.16; 120.19;
130.14; 133.14; 142.11; 143.
5; ds. life 18.16; 60.12; 72.18;
80.6; 90.5; 121.3; 129.8; as.
lif 8.4; 45.11; 72.14; 76.7;
77.7; 79.14; 80.6; 103.14; 130.
6; 136.16.

lifer sf. *jecur*, as. lifre 29.11.

liflic adj. *vitalis, vividus, vivus,*
nsm. dsn. liflic 92.7; liflicum

80.11; asf. liflic 14.6; gpm.
liflicra 98.10.

lig sm. *flamma*, ap. ligas 17.7;
lias 10.14.

ligen adj. *flammeus*, asn. ligen
22.11.

lilie wf. *lilium*, gs. lilian 135.9;
ap. lilian 140.5.

lim sn. *membrum*, np. lima 137.
6; ap. lima 79.2.

lið sn. *artus*, dp. liðum 14.10;
103.17; ap. liða 2.5; liðe 70.
7; lið 137.4.

liðe adj. *mitis, serenus,* nvsmn.
liðe 71.4; 77.12; 143.1; 145.
10; dsm. liðan 22.6; asn. liðe
24.7; apm. liðe 77.14; sup.
vsm. liðesta 65.6; 126.1.

lof sn. *laus, melos,* ns. 35.13;
45.17; 45.18; 46.1; 49.15;
55.10; 56.15; (Godes lof=
Alleluia) 77.15; 93.11; 94.
18; 96.10; 97.6; 98.2; 118.
17; 134.17; 146.6; ds. lofe 27.
9; 58.9; 62.12; 68.12; dp. lof-
um 57.1; 57.4; 57.7; 57.17;
58.4; 105.1; 122.1; 140.10;
147.3; ap. lofu 5.16; 43.4; 48.
4; 57.12; 60.16; 72.9; 86.17;
111.19; 115.2; 120.5; 123.10;
129.11; 134.3; 135.5; 145.2.

lofbære adj. *hymnifer*, dpn. lof-
bærum 57.6.

lofsang sm. *canticum, hymnus,*
ns. 146.5; ds. lofsange 40.3;
141.19; as. 2.12; 33.4; 40.
7; 45.1; 45.2; 69.3; 87.1;
108.6; 137.10; 139.16; 141.
3; 144.4; np. lofsanges 87.2;

dp. lofsangum 29.7; ap. lof-
sangas 7.19; 26.3; 73.16; 140.
12.

losigan wv. *deperire, perimere,
perire,* ind. pres. 3 pl. losiað
141.14; pret. 3 sg. losode 90.
10; losede 142.5; inf. 34.11;
pres. p. dsm. losigendum 143.7.

lufigan wv. *diligere,* ind. pres. 3
pl. lufigað 13.2 ; opt. pres. 3
sg. lufige 2.15.

luflic adj. *amabilis,* nsm. 38.2.

lufu sf. *amor, caritas,* ns. lufe
2.15; ds. lufe 36.6; 70.8; 94.
4; 133.18; as. lufe 92.14; vs.
83.17.

lustbǣre adj. *libens,* nsm. lust-
bære 54.17.

lustlice adv. *libenter,* 137.10.

lūtigan wv. *latere,* pres. p. gpf.
lutigendra 33.13.

lȳdenwaru smpl. *Latini,* np.
lydenwaru 97.2.

lyft sn. *aer,* ds. lyftum 25.4; ap.
lyftu 66.3.

M

mǣden sn. *puella, virgo,* nvs.
mæden 54.10 (2); 75.9; 76.12;
77.11; 108.3; 110.9; 111.13;
139.2 (2); 139.5; 140.3; gs.
mædenes 27.6; 34.17; 41.4;
43.14; 44.1; 50.11; 75.6; 89.
10; 112.9; 119.3; 139.1; 139.
3; ds. mædene 39.11; 40.9; 50.
4; 87.7; as. mæden 53.2; 76.7;
np. mædena 140.9; gp. mædena
111.13; 119.17; 140.1; 140.6.

mǣdenlic adj. *virginalis, virgineus,* nsf. mædenlice 118.11;
dsmn. mædenlicum 108.5.

mægen sn. *virtus, vis,* ns. 47
16; gp. mægena 62.7; dp.
mægenū 7.18; 84.19; ap.
mægnu 6.13; mægenu 32.13.

mǣgð sf. *natio, tribus,* ds.
mægðe 42.16; np. mægðe 99.
6; dp. mægðum 78.15.

mænig adj. *multus,* apm. mænige
32.11.

mænigu wf. *turba,* ns. 97.8;
121.5; np. 94.6.

mænnisc, see mennisc.

mænnisclice, see mennisclice.

mǣrigan wv. *praestare,* pres. p.
dsm. mæregendiendum 46.2.

mǣrlice adv. *magnifice,* mærlice
47.16.

mǣrða sfpl. *magnalia,* ap.
mærða 96.18.

mǣst, see micel.

magan swv. *posse, quire, valere,*
ind. pres. 3 sg. mæg 33.8;
132.17; pret. 2 sg. mihtest
103.15; opt. pres. 3 sg. mage
90.6; mæge 32.19; 1 pl. magon 145.1; 3 pl. magon 102.1.

mān sn. *nefas, piaculum, probrum,*
as. mán 104.6; 115.11; dp.
manum 67.8; ap. man 5.10;
23.9.

mann sm. *homo,* nvs. 43.1; 83.
19; gs. mannes 28.5; 53.6;
ds. menn 45.7; 45.8; mann
28.12; as. mann 31.2; 31.13;
gp. manna 23.1; 132.10; 141.
16; ap. menn 32.5; 70.9.

manna wm. *homo*, as. mannan 42.11.

māra, see micel.

martyrdōm sm. *martyrium*, ds. martyrdome 38.8; 105.12.

mater sf. *mater*, ns. 55.14.

mēd sf. *praemium*, ns. med. 88. 10; gs. mede 67.1; ds. mede 83.2; as. mede 11.7; 14.6; 118. 16; 134.2; dp. medum 138.10; ap. meda 28.17; 140.8.

mennisc adj. *humanus*, gsn. mennisces 31.6; mænnisces 116.2.

mennisclice adv. *humanitus*, mænnisclice 90.15.

meolc sf. *lac*, ds. mcolce 51.5.

merig adj. *dulcis*, nsn. myrige 55.8; dsm. merigū 141.19; apm. merige 140.12.

mete sm. *cibus*, ns. mete 16.9; 58.5; gs. metes 9.12; dp. mettum 65.19.

micclum adv. *multum*, 62.10.

micel adj. *grandis*, *immensus*, *magnus*, nsn. 146.5; nsf. mycel 112.13; gsn. miceles 89. 5; dsn. miclum 136.6; vsm. 89.9; micele 25.1; 72.1; apm. micele 28.9; comp. nsf. mare 28.4; dsm. mæran 73.15; asm. mæran 103.1; sup. mvsm. mæsta 98.7; 104.11.

mid adj., asm. midne 60.1 (in phrase on midne dæg = *meridie*).

mid prep. w. dat. *cum* (216 times).

middæg sm. *meridies*, ns. 16.15; as. 10.13.

middaneard sm. *cosmus*, *mun-*

dus, ns. 4.2; 84.16; 96.6; 111. 7; 132.5; gs. middaneardes 9. 15; 19.14; 21.10; 29.4; 31.1; 34.14; 39.16; 49.2; 67.2; 79. 16; 89.3; 89.6; 91.11; 104.2; 104.20; 105.15; 122.6; 123. 15; 123.19; 126.12; 128.7; 130.2; 130.18; 134.5; 137.15; 138.7; midd'eardes 38.11; ds. middanearde 8.8; 47.4; 69.6; 86.8; 127.7; 143.7; middenearde 45.9; as. middaneard 34.12; 37.14; 75.13; 111.5.

middaneardlic adj. *mundanus*, apn. middaneardlice 74.2; 91.12.

mideard sm. *mundus*, gs. mideardes, 13.15.

miht sf. *numen*, *nutus*, *potentia*, *potestas*, *virtus*, nvs. 26.12; 35. 13; 47.1; 49.5; 49.16; 55. 4; 90.13; 105.5; 106.12; 114. 3; 114.16; 118.17; 125.8; 137. 13; gs. mihte 25.1; 52.15; 112. 8; ds. mihte 35.1; 35.4; 44. 16; 46.5; 61.8; 92.16; 115. 7; vs. myht 69.1; gp. mihta 42.1; 44.3; 72.3; 120.16; dp. mihtum 97.11; 123.2.

mihtelice adv. *potenter*, *potentialiter*, 26.2; mihtlyce 49.10; myhtylice 29.5.

mihtig adj. *polens*, nvsmf. 3. 15; 10.10; 42.5; 49.1; 68.2; nsm. mihtiga 104.16; gsf. mihtigre 15.18.

milde adj. *propitius*, nsm. mylde 53.10.

mildheort adj. *clemens*, nsm. 69. 4; 105.18; 124.9; 140.4; sup. vsm. mildheortesta 86.15.

mildheortlice adv. *clementer*, comp. mildheortlicor 138.1.

mildheortnyss sf. *clementia*, gs. mildheortnysse 29.3; 146.18; ds. mildheortnyssa 11.12; 115. 14.

miltsung sf. *indulgentia*, ds. miltsunge 37.11.

mislimp sn. *casus*, ap. 16.3.

mistlic adj. *diversus*, npf. mistlice 96.17; apf. mistlice 25.8.

mōd sn. *animus, mens*, ns. mod. 2.16; 10.5; 14.1; 16.16; 23. 13; 25.15; 25.16; 27.8; 37.5; 62.1; 63.2; 132.3; 132.15; gs. modes 7.12; 14.15; 20.3; 23.10; 30.6; ds. mode 21.18; 31.20; 70.4; 106.4; 125.12; 135.18; as. mod 3.5; 16.5; 70.1; 70.10; gp. moda 18.5; 18.15; 20.3; 23.2; 64.3; 66.11; dp. modum 104.21; 123.11; 129.12; 140.14; 145.1; ap. mod 2.7; 21.1; 92.2; 114.1; 127.3.

mōder sf. *mater, parens*, nvs. moder 75.11; 76.11; 103.10; 108.5; 109.1; 140.2; gs. 34. 17; 50.9; 112.12; 139.1; meder 51.1; ds. meder 87.7; as. moder 77.3; gp. moddra 52.3.

mōdig adj. *superbus*, nsf. modig 126.11.

mōdignyss sf. *superbia*, as. modignesse 9.11.

molde wf. *humus, solum*, as. moldan 17.8; 19.14; 28.7.

mōna wm. *luna*, ns. mona 35.6; 75.3; gs. monan 22.13.

mōnað sm. *mensis*, gp. monða 22.17.

mugan, see magan.

mundbyrd sf. *patrocinium*, dp. mundbyrdū 111.22.

munuc sm. *monachus*, gp. muneca 72.13; 110.11; 118.13; 119. 18.

murcnung sf. *murmur*, ns. 132. 14.

mūð sm. *os*, nvs. muð 10.5; 127.9; ds. muðe 15.5; 47.14; 76.15; 135.16; 141.2.

mycel, see micel.

myht, see miht.

myhtelice, see mihtelice.

mylde, see milde.

myrig, see merig.

myx sn. *faex*, ds. myxe 136.1.

N

nā adv. *ne, nec, non*, na 36.13; 37.15; 42.2; 43.17; 51.4; 51. 6; 61.16; 74.9.

nacod adj. *nudatus*, npm. nacode 130.11.

næddre wf. *serpens*, ns. 61. 16.

næfre adv. *nusquam*, næfre 11.6.

nægl sm. *clavus*, dp. næglum 78.5.

nænig indef. prn. *nemo*, nsm. nænig 33.8.

nāht indef. prn. *nihil*, nsn. naht 98.12; asn. naht 14.3; 24.9; 24.10.

nama wm. *cognomen, nomen*, ns. 47.8; gs. naman 62.12;

138.3; ds. naman 65.14; as. nama 76.17; 103.2; ap. naman 114.13.

nān prn. and adj. *nullus*, nsnf. nan 44.19; 142.13; 143.7; asm. nænne 25.13; 25.14; npf. nane 17.16; 143.5; dpfn. nanum 20.8; 27.2.

ne adv. *ne, non* (thirty-five times).

ne conj. *nec, -ve,* 24.12; 25.12; 25.16; 125.1; 132.14(2); 139.9(2).

nēadigan wv. *cogere*, ind. pres. 3 sg. neadað̆ 56.7; 84.9; 3 pl. neadiað̆ 56.2.

nēadwīs adj. *debitus*, nsn. neadwis 49.15; apmn. neadwise 27.10; 60.16; 86.17; 120.5; 123.10; 129.11; apn. neadwisa 91.19.

nēah adj. sup. *proximus*, apm. neoxtan 10.8.

neaht, see **niht**.

nearonyss sf. *arlum*, dp. nearonyssū 70.10.

neorxnewang sm. *Paradisus*, ds. neorxnewange 115.13; nearxnewange 64.5; nerxnewange 47.6; as. neorxnewange 135.11; neoxnewange 83.6.

nēowigan, see **nīwian**.

nēoxta, see **nēah**.

netan, see **nytan**.

niht sf. *nox*, nvs. 3.4; 14.19; 21.9; 23.5; 30.8; 44.18; 44.19; nyht 15.1; gs. nihte 2.10; 6.6; 8.10; 19.10; 20.18; 26.6; 30.5; 40.13; 61.13; neahte 12.6; ds.

nihte 4.7; 74.10; nyhte 6.8; 7.16; 12.10; as. nihte 2.4; 6.2; 9.14; 12.12; 27.16; 53.14; niht 18.3; nyht 6.8; np. nihta 143.6; gp. nihta 11.15; 27.13; nyhta 3.2; 29.15; dp. nihtum 21.2; 22.15; 26.10.

nihtes adv. *nocte*, 145.3.

nihtlic adj. *nocturnus*, nsn. nyhtlic 6.7; dsf. nyhtlicre 33.3.

niman sv. *assumere, sumere, tenere, tollere*, opt. pres. 3 sg. nime 14.6; 57.6; 77.4; nyme 37.8; imp. pl. nimað̆ 57.11; inf. 23.15; pres. p. nsf. nimende 76.14; npm. nimende 135.12; pp. pl. numene 32.3.

niðerāstīgan sv. *descendere*, ind. pret. 3 sg. nyðerastah 45.13; inf. niðerastigan 32.22.

nīðful adj. *invidus*, gsm. niðfulles 3.11.

nīwe adj. *novus*, nsn. niwe 37.7; 74.1; gsn. niwes 13.14; 17.11; 97.9; dsmn. niwum 87.3; 94.7; asm. niwne 40.7; asn. niwe 19.12; 44.18; 52.15; npn. niwa 136.7; npm. niwan 87.2.

nīwigan wv. pres. p. (*novus*), nsm. neowiende 97.17.

niwolnyss sf. *imum*, dp. niwolnyssum 2.13.

nōnsang sm. *nona*, as. nonsang 60.17.

nū adv. *jam, modo, nunc*, nu 1.13; 5.1; 5.20; 6.5; 8.10; 10.1; 17.9; 19.4; 29.16; 34.4; 36.5; 37.7; 38.2; 42.13; 46.10; 53.17; 56.5; 59.16; 64.9; 72.10; 73.16; 80.9; 87.2; 90.3; 91.4; 93.9; 93.14; 94.13; 97.15; 104.16;

105.18; 106.14; 108.10; 113.
8; 120.13; 124.5; 124.9; 131.1;
133.15; 136.13; 137.6; 137.9;
138.18; 139.14; 146.7; 146.12.

nyht, see **niht**.

nyhtlic, see **nihtlic**.

nyman, see **niman**.

nytan anv. *nescire*, opt. pres.
3 sg. nyte 3.3; 16.16; nete 16.
8; 20.10; inf. 25.11; 140.15;
pres. p. nsf. nytende 50.15; vsm.
netende 104.9.

O

ō interj. *O* (148 times).

of prep. w. dat. *de, ex* (forty-
eight times).

ofāceorfan sv. *amputare*, imp.
sg. ofaceorf 15.4.

ofer prep. w. acc. *super, supra*,
38.3; 75.20; 88.14; 108.4; 110.
10; 126.10; 127.2.

oferfǣreld sn. *transitus*, ds. ofer-
fǣrelde 82.3.

oferfell sf. *crapula*, ds. oferfelle
97.9.

oferhęligan wv. *contegere, detegere*,
ind. pres. 2 sg. oferhelast 12.6;
3 sg. oferhelað 23.5.

oferswiðan wv. *devincere, superare, vincere*, ind. pres. 2 sg.
oferswiðst 131.13; 133.9; pret.
2 sg. oferswiðdest 80.8; 84.10;
3 sg. oferswiðde 84.1; imp. sg.
oferswið 131.15; pres. p. nsm.
oferswiðende 79.8; 91.12; pp.
dsm. oferswiðdū 4.4; oferswið-
dan 130.3.

ofęstlice adv. *propere*, 86.4.

offrigan wv. *offerre*, imp. sg. offra
98.17; 113.12.

offrung sf. *victima*, as. offrunge
52.6.

ofhrēosan sv. *obruere*, opt. pres.
3 sg. ofhreose 18.8.

ofsęttan wv. *comprimere*, imp.
sg. ofsete 11.16.

ofslēan sv. *perimere*, gsf. ofslæg-
enne 103.6; dsm. ofslegenum
89.6.

oftrǣdlice adv. *frequenter, saepius*,
116.11; 137.5.

ofðriccan wv. *comprimere, deprimere, imprimere, reprimere*,
opt. pres. 3 sg. ofðricce 25.13;
3 pl. ofðreccan 17.16; imp. sg.
ofðrice 13.4; ofðrece 11.16;
pres. p. vsm. ofðriccende 25.5.

ōga wm. *horror, pavor, terror*, ns.
oga 3.12; 9.6; 37.14; ds. ogan
130.3.

olfend sm. *camelus*, ns. 103.16.

on prep. *in*, w. dat. (211 times);
w. acc. 1.13; 5.20; 12.3; 15.
6; 33.15; 34.4; 35.16; 40.11;
59.16; 83.14; 99.11; 118.20;
120.10; 124.8; 135.2; 138.18;
142.7; 146.7.

onǣlan wv. *accendere*, imp. sg.
onæl 92.13.

onāgēotan sv. *infundere*, imp. sg.
onageot 1.5.

onāginn sn. *primordium*, dp.
onaginnū 13.14.

onāsęndan wv. *infundere*, imp.

sg. onasend 15.15; onasænd
92.14; onasynd 17.9.

onāsēon sv. *illabi*, ind. pres.
3 sg. onasihð 30.2.

onāslīdan sv. *illabi*, ind. pres.
3 sg. onaslit 13.18; imp. sg.
onaslid 15.12; 53.10; pp. apf.
onaslíd 94.15.

onbæcgedōn anv. *retroagere*, pp.
apm. onbæcgedonne 65.3.

onbelǣdan wv. *irrogare*, pres. p.
vsm. onbelædende 25.6.

onbyrgan wv. *gustare*, pres. p.
dsn. onbyrgendum 82.8.

oncnāwan rv. *agnoscere, noscere*,
opt. pres. 1 pl. oncnawan 93.4;
pp. dsm. oncnawenum 86.3.

ondrǣdan rwv. *timere*, ind. pres.
2 sg. ondrædst 51.14.

onfōn rv. *rapere, suscipere*, ind.
pret. 3 pl. onfengon 38.10; inf.
onfon 32.6.

ongēan prep. w. acc. *adversus,
contra*, ongean 80.15; 135.13.

ongēanbringan wv. *reducere,
referre*, ind. pres. 3 sg. ongean-
bringð 9.14; pret. 3 sg. ongean-
brohte 59.8; 93.17; imp. sg.
ongeanbring 47.14; inf. ongean-
hringan 47.10.

ongēancuman sv. *occurrere*, ind.
pret. 3 sg. ongeancom 97.12.

ongēancyme sm. *recursus, regressus*, ns. ongeancyme 44.
10; 44.12.

ongēangecyrran wv. *egredi, revertere*, pp. pret. ongeangecyrryd
7.6; nsm. ongeangecyrred 95.2.

ongēangehwyrfan wv. *redire*, inf.
ongengehwyrfan 61.13.

ongēansęndan wv. *refundere,
remittere*, ind. pres. 2 sg. ongean-
sændst 25.3; pp. ongeangesend
7.4.

ongebringan wv. *ingerere*, imp.
sg. ongebring 19.12; pp. onge-
broht 10.3.

onginnan sv. *capere, templare*,
ind. pres. 2 sg. onginst 91.17;
opt. pres. 3 sg. onginne 61.17.

onhrēosan sv. *irruere*, opt. pres.
3 sg. onhreose 12.13.

onlēohtan wv. *inlucere, inluminare, inlustrare*, ind. pret. 3 sg.
onleohte 89.2; opt. pres. 3 sg.
onleohte 27.14; imp. sg. onleoht
22.6; 23.1; 36.5; 113.7; pres.
p. vsm. onleohtende 15.11.

onrǣs sm. *impetus*, ds. onræse
83.9.

onryne sm. *cursus*, ds. 36.4.

onsǣgednyss sf. *hostia, victima*,
nvs. onsægednyss 78.8; 79.11;
82.17; ds. onsægednysse 59.6;
vs. onsægednyssa 80.10; dp.
onsægednyssum 65.8; ap. onsægednysse 98.17.

onsīgan sv. *urgere, vergere*, ind.
pret. 3 sg. onsah 96.1; pres. p.
dsm. onsigendū 34.14.

onswēgan wv. *insonare*, opt. pres.
3 sg. onswege 9.6.

ontęndan wv. *accendere*, opt.
pres. 3 sg. ontende 10.8.

onwunigan wv. *instare*, ind. pres.
3 sg. onwunað 56.8; opt. pres.
3 sg. onwunige 11.8; 26.14.

openlice adv. *palam*, 51.9.

ordfruma wm. *origo*, as. ordfrum-
an 13.15; 42.18; 52.18.

ormǣte adj. *gigas, ingens, immensus*, nvs. ormǣte 17.1; 19.13; 44. 7; 145.5; 145.15; nsm. ormǣde 112.11.

orsorh adj. *tulus*, asmn. 77.8.

orðigan wv. *spirare*, pres. p. nsm. orðiende 98.9.

oð prep. *ad, in, usque*, w. dat. 46. 16; w. acc. 24.18; 50.2.

ōðer adj. *alius, alter, ceterus*, nsm. oðer 105.16; 105.16; npm. oðre 103.20; dpm. oðrum 118. 7; ap. oðre 73.3; 104.12.

ōðer sīðan adv. *secundo*, oðer sīðan 37.13.

oððæt conj. *donec*, 106.5; 125. 13.

oððe conj. *aut, vel*, 4.3; 5.5; 22. 15; 28.15; 28.16; 142.13.

P

pǣtig adj. *callidus*, nsf. wǣtige [i.e. pǣtige] 61.16.

picen adj. *piceus*, nsf. 142.15.

R

racentēg(e) wsf. *catena*, ap. racentegan 85.2; racentega 99.3.

rǣdgift sm. *senatus*, as. rǣdgyft 105.17.

rǣscan wv. *vibrare*, pres. p. dsn. rǣscendum 94.1.

rēad adj. *roseus, ruber*, gsf. readre 82.3; dsn. readum 82.7; 133.1.

rēadigan wv. *rubescere*, ind. pret. 3 pl. readodon 52.16; inf. readian 49.9; pres. p. dsn. readiendū 91.17.

rēaflāc smn. *praeda, rapina*, ns. rēaflāc 142.5; as. rēaflāc 79.6.

reccend sm. *rector*, vs. reccend 2.2; 10.10; 72.1; 116.2.

regol sm. *regula*, gs. regoles 70. 10; as. 61.3.

rene, see ryne.

rest sf. *requies*, ns. rest 12.11; 58.5.

rēðe adj. *dirus, ferox, saevus*, nsmn. reðe 142.5; dsf. reðre 47. 9; asm. reðan 113.13; npm. reðe 85.14; apnf. reðe 80.2; 132.10; 139.10.

rēðnyss sf. *ferociā*, ap. reðnyssa 132.9.

rīce sn. *regnum*, gs. rices 88.8; as. rice 36.12; 43.3; 116.4; ap. ricu 8.17; 38.12; 51.16; 55.3; 120.18.

rif sn. *alvus*, ns. 44.1; ds. rife 51. 1; as. 75.18.

riht adj. *rectus*, vpm. rihte 19.3.

rihtlice adv. *rite*, 92.11; 104. 22; 108.10; 134.7; 138.7; 141.9.

rihtwīs adj. *justus*, nsm. rihtwis 33.18; 54.13; vsm. rihtwisa 23.8; rihtwise 126.9; 128.9; dpm. rihtwisum 36.12; 113.6; vpm. rihtwise 122.5.

rihtwīsnyss sf. *justitia*, ns. rihtwisnyss 135.19.

rind sf. *cortex*, ds. rinde 79.7.

rīð smf. *rivulus*, dp. riðum 17.6.

rīxigan wv. *regnare*, ind. pres. 2 sg. rixast 125.10; 3 sg. rixað 12.4; 72.8; 91.8; 121.6; 3 pl. rixiað 117.7; pret. 3 sg. rixode 78.16; inf. rixian 49.14; pres. p. nsm. rixiende 108.16.

rōd sf. *crux*, gs. rode 59.7; 78. 2; 79.18; 80.16; 82.6; ds. rode 53.3; 89.11; as. rode 32.5; 32. 14; 38.16; 80.3; 105.16.

rodor sm. *aether, Olympus*, gs. rodores 108.4; roderes 55.2; ds. rodore 56.13; 91.10; 102. 5; 108.15; rodere 37.4; 48.6; np. roderas 74.16.

rodorlic adj. *aethereus*, nsm. roderlica 118.6; npm. rodorlice 57.2.

rōsen adj. *roseus*, dsm. rosenum 105.10.

rūh adj. *yrcus* [=*hirtus*], asm. ruhue 103. 16.

ryue sm. *cursus, recursus*, ap. rynas 16.17; renas 22.14.

rẏnelīc adj. *mysticus*, gsm. rynelices 87.5; asn. rynelice 48.12.

rẏnelice adv. *mystice*, rynelice 68.7.

S

sācerd sm. *sacerdos*, vs. sacerd 98.17; gp. sacerda 118.10.

sacu sf. *lis*, gs. sace 9.6; 29.1; gp. saca 10.14.

sǣ smf. *mare, pontus*, ns. sǣ 39. 17; gs. sǣs 6.14; sǣ 76.10; 82.3.

sǣd sn. *semen*, ds. sǣde 42.2; 43. 17; ap. sǣd 75.8.

sǣlig adj. *felix*, nsm. sǣliga 48.17.

samod adv. *pariter, simul, una*, 8.1; 8.3; 8.6; 17.6; 35.15; 38. 14; 46.17; 69.3; 72.7; 73.9; 105.2; 105.14; 113.15; 114.13; 116.15; 117.2; 118.19; 120.1; 120.9; 120.11; 125.9; 133.3; 135.1; 141.3; 141.18; 145.7; 146.1.

samodārīsan sv. *consurgere*, ind. pres. 1 pl. samodarisað 26.5.

samodbecuman sv. *confugere*, pres. p. dpm. samodbecumendū 109.4.

samodblissigan wv. *congaudere, conlaetari*, opt. pres. 3 sg. samodblissige 28.3; 1 pl. samodblissigan 77.10.

samodgęddung sf. *consonus*, ds. samodgeddunge 109.11.

samodgehęrigendlic adj. *conlaudabilis*, asm. samodgeherigendlicne 109.10.

samodhęrigan wv. *conlaudare*, ind. pres. 1 pl. samodherigað 115.3.

samodhlēoðrigan wv. *concinere*, ind. pres. 1 pl. samodhleoðriað 40.7.

sang smn. *cantus, concentus*, ds. sange 73.7; dp. sangum 57.9; 132.3.

sār sn. *dolor*, dp. sarum 85.8.

sāwul sf. *anima*, ns. sawul 31. 18; gs. sawle 13.9; np. sawle 73.8; ap. saula 73.4.

scaða wm. *latro*, gs. scaðan 7.5.

sceadu sf. *umbra*, ns. 8.10; ap. sceaduwa 142.8.

scefe sm. *praeceps*, ds. 24.5.

scęncan wv. *propinare*, pres. p. nsm. scencende 31.8.

scēp sn. *bidens, ovis*, as. scēp 59.8; gp. scepa 132.13; ap. scép 98.15; 103.17.

sceppend, see scyppend.

scētefinger sm. *index*, ds. scetefingre 104.3.

scettels sm. *sera*, ap. scettelsas
122.10.

scildig, see scyldig.

scīnan sv. *clarere, coruscare, effulgere, florescere, fulgere, lucere,
micare, nitere, promicare, radiare, refulgere, relucere, resplendere, splendere*, ind. pres. 2 sg.
scinst 108.1; 3 sg. scinð 8.11;
27.11; 37.4; 37.7; 37.13; 44.
17; 47.8; 114.2; 3 pl. scinað
44.3; 78.2; pret. 3 sg. scán 43.
20; 48.1; 66.8; 74.1; 74.7; 74.
10; 86.8; 93.19; 138.4; opt.
pres. 3 sg. scine 3.4; 44.20;
imp. sg. scin 7.11; inf. scinan
91.18; pres. p. (*candidus, fulgidus, lucidus, nitidus, splendidus*)
nvs. scinende 15.13; 35.7; 48.
5; 48.6; 78.17; 80.10; 85.10;
98.4; 108.15; 127.2; sgm. scin-
endes 21.16; dsmn. scinendum
86.12; 114.2; 121.2; dsf. scin-
endre 114.11; asm. scinendne
22.8; asn. scinende 74.14; dpm.
scinendum 82.2; 133.2; apf.
scinende 88.4; vpm. scinende
119.14.

scīnhīw sn. *monstrum*, ns. scin-
hiw 142.6.

scippend, see scyppend.

scop sm. *vates*, gp. scopa 54.5;
vp. scopas 119.9.

scrǣf sn. *antrum*, ap. scrǣfu
103.12.

scucca wm. *zabulus* [= *diabolus*],
as. scuccan 115.8.

sculan anv. *debere*, ind. pres. 2
sg. scealt 68.4.

scūr sm. *nimbus*, np. scuras 142.
14.

scyld sm. *clipeus, scutum*, ds.
scylde 54.2; as. scyld 135.14.

scyld sf. *reatus, scelus*, ds. scylde
37.15; as. scylde 102.3; 104.
2; 133.12; gp. scylda 120.15;
scylde 144.7; ap. scylde 30.6;
56.6; 128.8.

scyldig adj. *reus*, dpm. scyldigum
34.13; 76.18; 105.13; apm.
scyldige 12.16; 125.4; 126.11;
scildige 2.11.

scypman sm. *nauta*, ns. 6.13.

scyppan sv. *formare*, pp. nsm.
sceapen 111.6.

scyppend sm. *conditor, creator,
plasmator*, nvs. 4.3; 6.1; 11.
11; 13.12; 17.1; 28.5; 30.14;
34.6; 51.10; 62.2; 72.7; 78.3;
83.18; 92.1; 112.10; vs. scippend 58.8; sceppend 2.1; 19.
13; 20.11.

sē pers. dem. rel. prn. and def.
art. *hic, ille, qui*, nsm. se (thirty
times); nsf. seo 1.4; 24.5; 31.
9; 57.9; 61.16; 68.9; 84.9; 96.
5; 117.2; 118.11; 121.6; 132.
17; 140.2; 140.3; nsn. ðæt 54.
5; 66.3; gsmn. ðæs (thirty
times); gsf. ðære 21.14; 22.12;
75.18; 78.9; 123.14; 126.5; 127.
2; 130.1; dsmn. ðam (sixty-
six times); dsm. ðæm 56.8;
ðan 44.13; 88.13; 143.13; dsf.
ðære 1.1; 4.13; 29.14; 32.15;
50.1; 59.5; 94.12; 113.8; 121.
4; ðæra 68.11; asm. ðone 4.
7; 4.8; 19.5; 77.9; 88.4; ðæne
8.13; 30.10; 31.5; 31.14;
31.17; 31.19; 33.8; 51.6; 53.
17; 54.13; 55.12; 65.12; 74.
16; 85.13; 108.9; 111.7; 113.
13; 116.10; 139.2; 140.2; 141.

18; ðænne 48.5; asf. ða (seven times); asn. ðæt(thirteen times); ismn. ðy 5.9; 26.17; 54.15; 134.13; ði 51.17; 125.2; np. ða (ten times); gp. ðæra 52.5; 122.13; 135.16; 135.17; 135. 18; 136.5; ðara 122.3; dp. ðam (eleven times); ap. ða (twenty-five times).

sealmsang sm. *psalmus*, dp. sealmsangum 7.17.

searu sn. *machina*, ns. seara 91. 1; gs. seares 29.4; as. seare 75. 1; 137.15.

sēcan wv. *quaerere, requirere*, ind. pret. 3 pl. sohton 52.1; inf. secan 4.7; 4.8; 23.16.

secgan wv. *asserere, dicere*, ind. pres. 1 pl. secgað 43.4; 57.15; pret. 3 pl. sædon 88.1; opt. pres. 1 pl. secgan 145.8; inf. secgan 85.20; pres. p. nsm. secgende 78.15; npm. secgende 60.17; 145.4.

sefa wm. *sensus*, dp. sefum 22.2; 53.11; 92.13; ap. sefan 114.8.

sēferlic adj. *sobrius*, asf. seferlice 16.11; npm. seferlice 19.6.

sēfernyss sf. *sinceritas*, gs. syfernysse 82.5.

sēfre adj. *sobrius*, nsmn. sefre 2.16; 27.8; 137.2; nsn. syfre 63.2; vpm. sefre 19.3.

sēl adj. sup. *optimus*, asn. selosta 132.4; vsm. selosta 20.11; sælosta 13.12.

selene sf. *donum*, ns. selene 92.6; as. selene 17.10; dp. selenum 4.16; 29.17; ap. selene 94.16; selenu 66.9.

self prn. *ipse, se*, nsm. 18.2; 72.16; 77.4; sylf 38.7; 111.11; 113.5; sylfa 6.15; nsf. selfe 84. 9; dsm. selfū 24.8; 73.12; 86. 11; selfon 74.3; asn. 14.4; npm. selfe 5.8; 9.16; sylfe 5. 14; apm. selfe 24.5.

sellan wv. *dare, donare*, ind. pres. 2 sg. selst 6.3; 3 sg. selð 51. 16; 105.13; 1 pl. sellað 115.2; pret. 2 sg. sealdest 19.16; 28. 12; 31.4; 32.7; 3 sg. sealde 22.18; 52.11; opt. pres. 2 sg. selle 56.13; 92.18; 133.5; 3 sg. selle 8.16; 60.9; sylle 16.4; 127.12; imp. sg. sele 63.1; 88. 5; 93.3; 93.10; syle 27.7; 28. 17; 28.18; 144.7; inf. sellan 37.12; 126.8; ger. to sellenne 95.4; pres. p. nsm. sellende 33. 16; syllende 53.8; 66.12; 131. 16; npn. syllende 136.8.

sellend sm. *largitor, lator*, nvs. syllend 66.2; 67.1.

sendan wv. *fundere*, imp. sg. sænd 76.16.

senfull adj. *peccator*, apm. synfullan 42.8.

sengigan wv. *peccare*, ind. pret. 1 pl. sengodon 21.8; 62.10; opt. pres. 3 pl. syngian 24.13.

senn sf. *lapsus, peccamen, peccatum*, gs. senne 105.19; 124. 10; 128.11; synne 126.3; ds. synne 46.13; as. senne 19.11; 30.6; 128.3; dp. sennum 118. 12; 122.11; ap. senna 52.9; 93.9; syuna 49.2.

sēoc adj. *aeger, languidus*, dpm. seocum 62.13; 136.9; 142.1; apm. seoce 123.1.

seofonfeald adj. *septemplex, septiformis*, gsf. seofonfealdre 92.9; dsf. seofonfealdre 96.2.

seofonsiðan adv. *septies*, seofonsiðan 96.3.

serwian wv. *insidiare*, pres. p. apm. serwiendan 13.4.

serwung sf. *insidia*, ap. syrwunga 47.13.

sē ðe rel. prn. *qui, quique*, nsm. se ðe (fifteen times); nsf. seo ðe 65.1; 90.15; asm. ðæne ðe 15.1; 50.18; 51.1; np. ða ðe (six times); ap. ða ðe (eleven times).

setl sn. *sedes*, ds. setle 39.15; 44.12; 89.12; 114.2; dp. setlum 4.12.

setlgang sm. *occasus*, as. 35.5; 61.12.

settan wv. *ponere*, inf. settan 104. 23.

sibb sf. *pax*, ns. sib 99.9; gs. sibbe 29.2; 113.14; 114.10; 116.5; ds. sibbe 76.16; 135.8; as. sibbe 10.17; 92.18; 133.5.

sīde wf. *latus*, gs. sidan 128.5.

sidefull adj. *pudicus*, nsm. 137. 1.

sige sm. *triumphus, trophaeum*, ns. 90.11; ds. 44.14; 84.7; 87. 12; 89.5; 134.15; as. 79.10; 106.15; 139.3; ap. sigas 47. 10; 129.10; 131.11.

sigefæst adj. *victor, victrix*, ns. 83.4; 84.7; 85.6; 133.10; sygefæst 66.6; sigefæste 47. 10; gs. sigefæstes 89.8; gp.

sigefæstra 132.4; vp. sigefæstan 58.2.

sīgelēan sn. *bravium*, ds. sigeleane 129.8.

sigorigan wv. *triumphare*, ind. pres. 3 sg. sigorað 123.19; 130. 18; pret. 3 sg. sigerode 105.16; pres. p. nsm. sigoriende 85.5; 133.9.

sigorlic adj. *triumphalis*, vpm. sigorlīce 123.13; 129.14.

sigriend sm. *victor*, ns. 38.3.

simbel sn. *sollemnis*, ns. 96.1.

simbelnyss sf. *sollemne*, np. symbelnyssa 122.4; ap. simbelnyssa 138.6.

simle adv. *semper*, 70.11; symle 7.17.

singal adj. *jugis, sedulus*, nsm. 58.2; dsf. singalre 88.5; dp. singalum 44.20; 127.6.

singan sv. *canere, cantare, psallere, resonare*, ind. pres. 3 sg. singð 137.10; 1 pl. singað 4.15; 18.12; 33.4; 56.14; 60.17; 114.18; 139.3; 144.4; 146.2; syngað 26.4; 3 pl. singað 51.8; 55.12; opt. pres. 3 sg. singe 121.5; 1 pl. singan 5.16; 9.16; 72.10; 3 pl. singan 122.4; imp. pl. singað 57.2; inf. 7.18; 45.1; 56.5; 59.4; 61.5; 72.5; 82.4; 87.1; 115.17; 123.11; 129.12; pres. p. npm. singende 2.12; 8.1; 18.3; 22.1; 60.16; 73.15; 123.10; 129.11; 140. 11; dpm. singendum 14.12; apm. singende 134.3.

siðfæt smn. *iter, semila, trames,* ds. siðfæte 87.3; as. siðfæt 77. 8; 104.10; 114.10.

siððau adv. *dein, post, posthinc,* 36.9; 70.5; 127.8; syððan 70.9.

sittan sv. *residere, sedere,* ind. pres. 2 sg. sitst 84.8; 3 sg. sitt 55.6; 105.7; sytt 60.8; inf. 88.7; pres. p. nvsm. sittende 108.3; 128.10; 137.14.

slæge sm. *caedes,* ds. 47.13.

slæp sm. *somnus, sopor, soporus,* ns. slæp 12.13; gs. slæpes 2.4; 3.8; ds. slæpe 14.10; 19.2; 20. 14; as. slæp 7.12; 12.17; 19.9.

slæpan, see slāpan.

slæwð sf. *torpor,* ns. slæwð 26. 14; dp. slæpðum [i. e. slæwðum] 4.5.

slāpan rv. and wv. *dormire,* inf. slapan 3.5; 3.6; 19.8; pres. p. gpm. slæpendra 32.11.

slāpol adj. *somnolentus,* apm. slapolan 7.1.

slāpolnyss sf. *somnolentia,* as. slapolnyssa 18.7.

slāw adj. *torpidus,* nsn. slawe 37.5.

sleacgigan wv. *pigritari,* pres. p. apm. sleacgiendan 18.8.

slide sm. *lapsus,* as. 25.11; 128. 3; np. slidas 7.9.

slincend smn. *reptans,* gs. slincendes 28.8.

slipor adj. *lubricus,* nsf. 5.5; gsn. slipores 30.4; dsn. sliporū 3.9; asm. sliporne 15.19; npn. slipere 24.13.

slipornyss sf. *lubricum,* np. slipornysse 36.8.

slitan sv. *lacerare, mordere,* ind. pres. 3 sg. 23.14; pres. p. nsm. slitende 132.11.

smēagan wv. *meditari, rimari,* inf. smeagen 7.17; smegan 36.10.

smēagend sm. *scrutator,* vs. smeagend 62.6.

smęrung sf. *unctio,* ns. 92.8.

smilte adj. *serenus,* asn. 24.7.

snāhwīt adj. *niveus,* gsf. snawitre 104.9.

snoter adj. *prudens,* nsm. 137. 1.

sōð adj. *verus,* asm. soðne 48.11; asf. soðe 10.17; vsn. soðe 98. 5; vsf. soð 15.12; 145.15; vpn. soðe 105.15; 123.15; 130.2; soða 122.6.

sōðfæst adj. *verax,* vsm. soðfæsta 10.10.

sōðfæstnyss sf. *veritas,* ns. soðfæstnyss 135.19.

sōðlice adv. *vere, vero,* soðlice 82.17; 128.11; 141.15.

sōðlufu sf. *caritas,* ns. soðlufu 10.7; 28.4; 92.7; 114.4; 123. 18; 130.17; gs. soðre lufe 46. 5; 59.3; 106.9; ds. soðre lufe 94.4.

spātl sn. *sputum,* ap. spátlu 80.1; spatle 89.11.

spearnyss sf. *parcitas,* ns. spearness 9.12.

spēd sf. *ops,* ds. spede 117.14; as. spede 109.3; 113.14.

spere sn. *lancea,* gs. speres 78.10.

sprǣc sf. *famen, loquela, sermo,* gs. spræce 103.5; is. spræce 92.12; 103.15.

sprecau sv. *affari, alloqui, fari, loqui, probare,* ind. pret. 3 pl. spræcon 94.5; 96.18; 97.4; 97.13; 109.12; opt. pres. 1 pl. sprece 24.9; pres. p. npm. sprecende 87.9.

sprytting sf. *germen,* ds. spryttinge 76.2; as. sprettinge 19.17.

spurplætt sm. *colaphus,* ap. spurplættas 80.1.

stān sm. *lapis, petra,* ns. stan 6. 15; ds. stane 85.3; ap. stanas 104.17.

standau sv. *stare,* pres. p. npm. standende 87.6; 87.10.

stefn sf. *vox,* ns. 2.14; 7.13; 37.1; 49.3; 55.9; 55.16; 132. 17; gs. stefne 103.7; ds. stefne 86.14; 114.18; 145.7; as. stefne 37.12; np. stefna 96.17; 113. 18; dp. stefnum 19.5; 57.14; 58.11; 115.2; 115.16; 131.10; 138.2.

stēman wv. *redolere,* pres. p. vsm. stemenda 47.11.

stēopcild sn. *orphanus,* gp. steopcilda 145.16.

steorra wm. *stella,* nvs. 48.5; 76.10; as. steorran 51.18.

sterung sf. *motus,* ap. sterunga 20.6.

sticol adj. *arduus,* apm. sticole 89.4.

stīg sf. *collis,* ap. stige 104.19.

stille adj. *tacitus,* dsf. stilre 132. 15.

stilnyss sf. *quies,* ns. stilness 2.5; ds. stilnesse 20.13.

stōw sf. *locus,* ns. stow 142.9; as. stowe 17.5; 113.7; ap. stowa 25.8.

strǣle wf. *spiculum,* ns. stræle 30.3.

strǣngð sf. *robur, vigor,* ns. 10.5; 11.1; as. 66.11.

strang adj. *fortis, robustus,* nsm. 42.7; stranga 116.9; gsf. strangre 35.1; apm. strange 106.8; sup. nsm. strængesta 84.18.

stranglic adj. *fortis, strenuus,* apf. stranglice 16.1; 132.2.

stranglice adv. *fortiter,* 132.11; 134.9; 135.15.

strēow sn. *foenum,* ds. streowe 51.3.

sūcan sv. *lactare,* ind. pres. 2 sg. sycst 75.22.

sum indef. prn. *quidam,* apm. sume 104.13.

sunne wf. *sol,* nvs. 1.4; 15. 12; 35.5; 61.12; 86.8; sunna 75.3; gs. sunnan 21.14; 22.12; 50.1; 127.2.

sunu sm. *filius, genitus, natus, partus,* ns. 30.16; suna 16. 19; 33.21; 124.3; 130.21; gs. suna 8.6; 109.2; ds. suna 1.11; 10.2; 35.14; 45.5; 45.18; 46. 17; 93.11; 94.18; 96.10; 97.6; 98.2; 120.8; 134.18; sunan 43.5; 118.18; as. suna 43.2; 50.16; 65.11; 66.13; 93.4; 108. 14; 109.6; 109.9; 133.8; 141. 18.

swā adv. *sic, tam, tanto, ut,* swa 1.14; 3.17; 5.21; 8.9; 17.14; 18.9; 24.11; 34.5; 39.13; 43·

10; 45.8; 46.2; 47.15; 56.16;
62.14; 63.8; 65.15; 79.2; 83.
15; 88.1; 93.1; 93.15; 105.9;
110.3; 115.21; 118.21; 135.3;
137.7; 145.9; 147.5.

swæc sm. *sapor*, as. 79.8.

swā hwā indef. pers. prn. *quisquis*, asn. swa hwæt 26.9.

swā hwā swā indef. pers. prn. *quisquis*, asn. swa hwæt swa 28.14; 30.7.

swā hwider swā adv. *quocunque*, swa hwider swa 140.9.

swā hwile indef. pers. prn. *quislibet*, dsf. swa hwilcre 137.7.

swār adj. *gravis*, dsm. swarran 13.8.

swā swā adv. *quemadmodum, sicut, ut, velut*, swa swa 4.8; 5. 15; 16.14; 16.15; 21.2; 34.15; 42.13; 45.3; 45.4; 45.5; 45.6; 74.1; 88.2; 93.13; 112.7.

sweart adj. *ater, taeter*, nsmf. 13.18; 23.5; gsf. sweartre 40. 13; dpn. sweartū 142.15; apn. swearte 112.14.

swefn sn. *somnium*, np. swefna 11.14; ap. swefnu 37.3.

swefnigan wv. *somniare*, opt. pres. 3 pl. swefnian 3.10.

swēgan wv. *concrepare, intonare, personare, persultare, resonare, resultare, sonare*, ind. pres. 3 sg. swegð 6.5; 37.1; 47.8; 52. 3; 57.9; 84.15; 96.6; 141.6; 3 pl. swegað 73.7; 87.2; 140.12; pret. 3 sg. swegde 110.3; 132. 14; 3 pl. swegdan 96.17; opt. pres. 3 sg. swege 2.14; 7.13; 10.6; 30.3; 121.5; 122.2; 141. 17; 1 pl. swegan 139.15; inf.

swegan 102.1; 115.16; pres. p. nsn. swegende 57.6.

swētnyss sf. *balsamum*, ap. swetnyssa 98.9.

swētswēge adj. *suavisonus*, dpn. swetswegū 58.8.

swīge wf. *silentium*, ds. swigean 40.13.

swilc adj. *talis*, nsf. 43.16; dsn. swilcum 90.5.

swilce, see ēac swilce.

swingel wf. *flagrum, verber*, ap. swingla 80.2; 88.11; 132.10.

swīðe adv. *nimis*, swiðe 72.17; sup. (*maxime*) swiðost 23.18; 106.8.

swīðorwillan anv. *malle*, pres. p. nsm. swiðorwillende 70.6.

swīðre adj. in comp. *dexter*, nsf. swiðra 13.1; gsf. swiðran 92. 10; dsf. swiðran 84.8; 90.12; swiððran 80.9; asf. swiðran 4. 10; 27.7.

swīðrigan wv. *valere*, inf. swiðrian 70.2; pres. p. nsm. swiðrigende 70.3.

swūra wm. *collum*, ap. swuran 70.12.

swurd sn. *ensis, gladius, mucro*, ns. 7.5; ds. swurde 78.10; 98.16; 105.16; as. 135.14; dp. swurdū 132.13.

swutol adj. *notus, publicus*, dsf. swutolre 86.14; sup. asn. swuteloste 22.18.

sȳfernyss, see sēfernyss.

sȳfre, see sēfre.

sygefæst, see sigefæst.

sylf, see self.

syllan, see sellan.

syllend, see sellend.

symbelnyss, see simbelnyss.

symle, see simle.

synfull, see senfull.

syngian, see sengian.

synn, see senn.

syrwung, see serwung.

syðōan, see siðōan.

syttan, see sittan.

T

tācen sn. *signum*, ds. tacne 61.
4; 61.14; as. taen 22.18; dp.
tacnum 72.15; 73.1; 97.11.

tācenbora wm. *signifer*, vs. tacen-
bora 113.1.

tēar sm. *fletus, lacrima*, dp. tearum
37.12; 65.2; 128.2.

teart adj. *asper*, apn. tearte 16.3.

teartlice adv. *acriter*, comp. teart-
licor 5.8.

tellan wv. *deputare*, ind. pres. 3
pl. tellað 94.7.

tempel sn. *templum*, ns. 50.14;
gs. temples 32.9; 143.4; ds.
temple 44.4; as. 116.11.

tēon sv. *attrahere, instruere, trahere*, ind. pres. 2 sg. tihst 10.12;
pret. 3 sg. teah 24.6; 70.16;
pres. p. nsm. teonde 69.6.

tēonfeald adj. *deni*, dpm. teon-
fealdū 48.13; 104.12.

tīd sf. *hora, tempus*, ns. tid 96.
5; gs. tide 36.4; 143.12; ds.
tide 4.14; 26.6; 33.3; 35.11; 73.
14; 86.18; 93.6; 94.10; 121.7;
139.20; tida 59.5; as. tid. 33.
15; np. tida 141.8; gp. tidena
6.3; 60.15; 83.19; dp. tidum 4.
15; 61.11; 145.3; ap. tida 6.3;
11.3; 29.15; 61.13; 75.4; 93.
10; 96.4.

tihtan wv. *suggerere*, ind. pres.
3 sg. tiht 28.15.

tima wm. *tempus*, ns. tima 56.8;
as. timan 106.16.

tiðigan wv. *annuere, praestare*,
opt. pres. 3 pl. tiðian 118.15;
imp. sg. tiða 80.17.

tō prep. .w. dat. *ad*, to (thirty-
four times).

tōbecuman sv. *advenire*, ind.
pres. 3 sg. tobecymð 123.3.

tōbrecan sv. *confringere, frangere, rumpere*, ind. pres. 1 pl.
tobrecað 20.18; tobrycað 18.
3; 29.16; imp. sg. tobrec 19.
10; pp. pl. tobrecene 82.18;
dpn. tobrecenū 84.19.

tōbretan, see tōbrytan.

tōbringan wv. *conferre*, ind. pret.
3 sg. tobrohte 45.11.

tōbrycan, see tōbrecan.

tōbrytan wv. *atterere, conterere,
terere*, opt. pres. 3 sg. tobryte
9.11; 17.12; tobrete 17.15; 20.
6; pres. p. asm. tobrytendne
115.8; pp. tobrytt 62.14.

tōcwīsan wv. *quatere*, opt. pres.
3 sg. tocwise 142.13.

tōcyme sm. *adventus*, gs. tocymes
40.2.

tōdæg adv. *hodie*, todæg 136.19.

tōdǣlan wv. *dividere*, pres. p.
nsm. todælende 17.3.

tōdāl sn. *diremptio*, gs. todales 22.16.

tōgelȳsan wv. *solvere*, ind. pres. 2 pl. togelysað 122.10.

tōgeȳcan wv. *adaugere*, imp. sg. togeyc 140.14.

tōgetēon sv. *trahere*, ind. pret. 3 pl. togetugon 38.12.

tōgeðeodan wv. *adhaerere*, pres. p. npm. togeðeodende 61.6.

tōgyfes adv. *gratis*, togyfes 37. 10; 126.8.

tō hwī adv. *quid*, to hwi 51.14; 87.10.

tōlǣtan sv. pp. (*laxus*) dpf. tolætenū 102.1.

tōlȳsan wv. *absolvere, dissolvere, exsolvere, resolvere, solvere*, ind. pres. 3. sg. tolysð 6.10; pret. 2 sg. tolysdesd 125.2; 3 sg. tolysde 59.12; 85.2; 112.15; opt. pres. 3 sg. tolyse 2.8; 99.3; 1 pl. tolesan 7.14; 3 pl. 118.8; 120. 15; imp. sg. tolys 23.3; 29.1; 76.18; 102.3; 106.1; 124.11; 125.4; 128.11; 133.17; 134.4; toles 19.11; 72.12; pp. nsm. tolysed 7.10; 90.10; np. tolysede 124.16; 133.15; dp. tolysedum 85.7; 97.18; ap. tolysede 77.13.

tōsceacan sv. *discutere, dissicere*, imp. sg. tosceac 7.12; 19.9.

tōslītan sv. *scindere*, pp. ns. tosliten 32.9; toslitan 21.13.

tōslūpan sv. *solvere*, pp. apm. toslopene 2.5.

tōstencan wv. *dissipare*, opt. pres. 3 sg. tostence 17.8.

tōteran sv. *carpere, lacerare*, ind. pret. 3 sg. totær 132.11; pp. apm. totoran 125.1.

tōð sm. *dens*, ap. teð 16.2.

tōðindan sv. *tumescere*, ind. pret. 3 sg. toðand 44.1.

tōweard adj. *adfuturus, fulurus, venturus*, nsf. toweard 88.10; dsf. toweardre 74.8; 104.1; asm. toweardne 88.1; vsm. towearde 35.10; apn. towearde 119.8.

tōweorpan sv. *diruere*, ind. pret. 3 pl. towurpon 142.14; pres. p. nsm. towurpende 80.5.

tōwundorlic adj. *admirabilis*, asm. towundorlicne 109.9.

trendel sm. *centrum*, as. 22.8.

trēow sn. *arbor, lignum*, gs. treowes 31.7; ds. treowe 78.16; vs. treow 78.17.

trep sm. *acies*, ap. trepas 47.9.

trum adj. *firmus*, nvsf. 114.4; 145.14.

tuddor sn. *pignus, proles*, as. 49. 3; ns. 27.6; 108.2; ap. tuddra 52.4.

tunge wf. *lingua*, ns. 10.5; 14. 14; 24.12; gs. tungan 94.2; ds. tungan 132.17; as. tungan 9.5.

tungel sn. *astrum, sidus*, nvs. 37.7; 74.1; 98.4; 127.1; gs. tungles 21.16; 22.5; ds. tungle 9.1; 14.19; np. tungla 76.3; gp. tunglena 22.14; 34.6; dp. tunglum 35.7; ap. tunglu 38.4; tungla 73.6; 75.20; 87.10; 88 14; 95.1.

tungelwītega wm. *magus*, np. tungelwitegan 51.17; ap. tungelwitegan 48.7.

tunglen adj. *sidereus*, gs. tunglenes 58.1.

tux sm. *dens,* dp. tuxum 130.8.

twęlfta num. adj. *duodeni,* dsn. twelftū 128.9.

twifeald adj. *bini, duplex, geminus,* gsf. twifealdre 106.9; dsn. tweofealdū 139.5; dsf. twifealdre 126.5; 127.5.

twīnian wv. pres. p. (*dubius*) nsm. twiniende 103.4.

tydderlic adj. *fragilis,* asm. tydderlicne 139.6.

tȳn wv. *imbuere, instruere,* ind. pret. 3 sg. tyde 70.9; imp. sg. ty 106.3; 125.11.

Ð

Ðā adv. and conj. *dum, tunc,* 38. 13; 87.5; 97.7.

Ðænne adv. and conj. *cum, dum, qua, tunc,* 3.1; 9.13; 30.12; 36. 9; 37.13; 37.16; 83.3; 84.18; 91.17; 96.5; 123.3; 136.9; Ðoñ 14.3; Ðanne 28.4. See also sē.

Ðæræfter adv. *post,* Ðæræfter 38. 10.

Ðærrihte adv. *protinus,* Ðærrihte 131.9.

Ðærrihtes adv. *protinus,* Ðærihtes 92.18; 113.17.

Ðærtōēcan adv. *insuper,* Ðærtoecan 78.9.

Ðæslic adj. *congruus,* dsn. Ðæslicum 29.12.

Ðæt conj. *ut,* 2.5; 3.1; 5.10; 9.13; 24.1; 31.15; 37.13; 63.2; 102. 1; 129.8.

Ðā hwīle conj. *dum,* 137.3.

Ðanc sm. *grates, gratia,* ap. Ðancas 2.9; 89.13; Ðances 27.10.

Ðanon adv. *inde, unde,* 64.7; 95.2; 139.9.

Ðā Ðā conj. *cum,* 93.18.

Ðā Ðe conj. *cum, dum,* 85.19; 86.9; 139.6.

Ðe rel. prn. *qui,* ns. 12.3; 33. 15; 85.9; 95.2; 137.3; as. 76.1; 92.4; 105.13; 131.12; 141.5; np. 32.3; ap. 26.4; 52.9; 78.13; 127.11; 127.12; 132. 18; 145.18; see ic Ðe, sē Ðe, Ðū Ðe.

Ðearle adv. *nimis, valde,* 47.3; 104.8; 144.2.

Ðēaw sm. *mos,* ds. Ðeawe 135.9; Ðcawa 132.13; gp. Ðeawa 80. 14; dp. Ðeawum 28.15; 123.1; ap. Ðcawas 106.3; 125.11.

Ðēn sm. *famulus, minister,* ns. Ðen 70.13; as. Ðen 80.7; np. Ðenas 72.10; 102.2; gp. Ðena 111.3; dp. Ðenum 73.1; 114.6; 133.5; ap. Ðenas 13.5; 43.7; 119.2; 143.2.

Ðēnigan wv. *ministrare,* opt. pres. 3 sg. Ðenige 72.3; pres. p. nsm. Ðenigende 22.13.

Ðēod sf. *gens,* gs. Ðeode 98.5; 98.16; ds. Ðeode 47.9; 97.1; as. Ðeode 120.3; np. Ðeoda 76.8; gp. Ðeoda 41.1; 43.13; 48.2; 137.17; dp. Ðeodum 75.17.

Ðēon sv. *pollere, vigere,* opt. pres. 3 sg. Ðeo 143.11; pres. p. nvsm. Ðeonde 48.14; 127.5.

Ðeorf sn. *azyma,* ns. wearf 82.15.

Ðēostor sn. *tenebrae,* np. Ðeostru 14.18; 21.9; dp. Ðeostrum 30.7;

31.9; 108.12; ðystrum 142.15;
ap. ðeostru 3.3; 12.6; 18.5;
21.9.

ðēow sm. *vernaculus*, ds. ðeowe
45.6.

ðēowa wm. *famulus, servus*, gp.
ðeowena 67.3; 111.14; dp.
ðeowū 28.13; ap. ðeowan 13.2.

ðēowigan wv. *deservire, servire*,
ind. pres. 3 pl. ðeowiað 75.4;
opt. pres. 3 pl. ðeowian 28.11;
145.18.

ðēowtlic adj. *servilis*, asm. ðeowt-
licne 50.6.

ðēowtling sm. *servulus*, dp.
ðeowtlingum 25.9; 134.16;
138.13; ap. ðeowtlingas 124.
7; 125.3; 131.3.

ðēs dem. prn. *hic, iste*, nsm.
ðes 16.13; 17.15; 47.6; 47.7;
47.10; 87.11; 97.15; 136.17;
ðæs 143.9; nsf. ðeos 54.9; 139.
5; 142.9; nsn. ðis 141.9; gsm.
ðises 4.14; 71.1; 138.8; 138.
11; 138.13; gsf. ðissere 73.17;
139.13; dsmn. ðisum 6.9; 6.
13; 6.15; 13.8; 42.10; 57.15;
62.4; 116.11; 134.15; 138.1;
ðysum 6.11; dsf. ðissere 12.10;
83.8; 116.5; asm. ðisne 39.17;
40.1; 88.2; 93.13; 109.9; 137.
10; ðysne 39.17; 111.9; ðesne
17.16; asf. ðas 47.14; asn. ðis
24.7; 64.4; np. ðas 94.9; 132.
5; 132.9; gp. ðissera 121.1;
124.14; 124.16; dp. ðisum 73.
9; 105.13; 124.1; 124.2; 124.
3; 130.19; 130.20; 130.21;
132.11; ðysum 65.13; ap. ðas
66.9; 114.12; 117.9; 120.13;
140.4; 146.12.

ðider adv. *illuc*, 88.5.

ðīn poss. prn. *tuus*, nsmfn.
ðin 31.1; 44.17; 77.6; 139.5;
141.6; gsmn. ðines 26.12; 40.
2; 62.12; 72.9; 124.18; 133.
16; 138.3; 143.3; gsf. ðinre
40.6; 41.2; 42.21; 133.11;
146.18; dsmn. ðinum 22.4;
26.18; 32.20; 40.4; 55.2; 80.
12; 84.12; 111.8; 111.19;
dsf. ðinre 31.3; 36.6; 46.
11; 65.4; 93.8; 115.13; asm.
ðinne 56.12; 69.5; asf. ðine
54.1; asn. ðin 32.7; 83.10;
124.17; npm. ðine 39.8; 72.
10; gp. ðinra 55.16; 89.22; 98.
7; 102.2; 120.11; 134.1; dp.
ðinum 20.7; 28.13; 73.8; 126.
4; 128.8; 128.12; 129.4; 129.
7; ap. ðine 13.5; 84.6; 98.15;
119.2; 125.3.

ðing sn. *res*, ns. 30.4; as.
14.7; 37.8; np. 35.2; 75.3;
94.9; 98.13; 145.18; gp. ðinga
2.1; 22.3; 34.8; 65.18; 89.1;
119.1; 120.11; 141.1; dp. ðing-
um 21.15; 119.16; ðingon 131.
8; 134.8; ap. ðing 3.15; 28.6;
74.4; 127.11; 127.12; 131.7;
146.12.

ðingigan wv. *intercedere, interpellare*, imp. sg. ðinga 111.20;
ðinge 127.6.

ðingrǣden sf. *intercessio, interventus, obtentus*, ds. ðingrædene
46.12; 139.13; dp. ðingræde-
num 126.4.

ðoden sn. *turbo*, ns. 142.13.

ðoligan wv. *carere, pati, perferre*,
ind. pres. 3 pl. ðoliad 129.3;
pret. 3 sg. ðolude 45.12; 51.3;
51.5; ðolode 79.13; pres. p.
nsm. ðoliende 48.16; ðoligende
84.3.

Ðonne, see Ðænne.

Ðoterigan wv. *ululare*, ind. pres. 3 sg. Ðotera ð 84.17.

Ðrēagan wv. *concrepare, corri-gere, increpare*, ind. pres. 3 sg. ðreað 7.1; 37.2; 77.10; opt. pres. 3 sg. ðreage 114.8.

Ðrēofeald adj. *trinus, triplex*, ns. ðreofeald 91.1; dsmn. ðreofealdum 60.14; 65.13; ðryfealdū 104.14; asm. ðryfealdne 75.1.

Ðreowa, see Ðriwa.

Ðridda num. adj. *tertius*, nsf. 96. 5; dsf. ðriddan 59.5.

Ðrilic, see Ðrylic.

Ðrinen, see Ðrynen.

Ðristlǣcan wv. *audere*, ind. pres. 1 pl. ðristlǣcað 111.17.

Ðriwa adv. *ter*, 48.13; 61.10; ðreowa 104.12.

Ðrosm sm. *chaos*, ns. 13.18.

Ðrote wf. *guttur*, ap. ðrotan 92. 12.

Ðrōwǣre sm. *martyr*, gs. ðrowǣres 106.15; 134.3; vs. ðrowǣre 47.11; 104.10; 133.7; np. ðrowǣras 130.7; gp. ðrowǣra 118.9; 129.10; 131.2; 131.5; dp. ðrowǣrum 131.13; 132.18; vp. ðrowǣres 119.13.

Ðrōwigan wv. *pati*, ind. pret. 2 sg. ðrowodest 80.2.

Ðrōwung sf. *passio*, gs. ðrowunge 59.6; 79.12.

Ðrȳ num. *trinus*, ds. ðrym 77. 18.

Ðryfeald, see Ðrēofeald.

Ðrylic adj. *trinus*, nvsm. ðrylic

29.6; 55.7; 103.8; asm. ðrylicne 146.16; vsf. ðrilic 133.3.

Ðrymsetl sn. *thronus*, ds. ðrymsetle 87.4; 113.18.

Ðrynen adj. *trinus*, nsm. ðrinen 137.16; nvsm. ðrynen 105.2; 115.19.

Ðrynnyss sf. *Trinitas*, nvs. 61.9; 68.10; 144.1; gs. ðrynnysse 26.1; ds. ðrynnysse 106.11; 121.4; ðrynnisse 1.1; 145.6; ðrynnesse 74.12; ðrynessa 49. 15; vs. ðrynnes 3.16; 56.11; 59.13; 60.13; 63.4; 80.17; 144. 6; 145.14; 147.1; ðrynes 146. 8; ðrynnys 1.2; 34.1.

Ðū pers. prn. *tu*, nvs. ðu *passim*; ds. ðe (seventy-seven times); as. ðe (sixty-eight times); nvp. ge 19.2; 87.10; 106.7; 122.5; 122.9; ap. eow 57.5; 57.8; 128.4.

Ðunigan wv. *exstare*, ind. pres. 3 sg. ðunað 4.2; ? ðuni... 28.4.

Ðurh prep. *per*, w. acc. (thirty-nine times).

Ðurhfaran sv. *penetrare, transire*, ind. pret. 3 sg. ðurhfor 112.6; 3 pl. ðurhforan 142.14; pres. p. nsm. ðurhfarende 84.5.

Ðurhfēre adj. *pervius*, nsn. ðurhfere 112.4.

Ðurhtēon sv. *conferre, conlegere*, opt. pres. 2 sg. ðurhteo 5.12; 3 sg. ðurhteo 9.7; 68.9; imp. sg. ðurhteoh 10.16.

Ðurhwacol adj. *pervigil*, nsm. 6.6.

Ðurhwunigan wv. *permanere*, ind. pres. 3 sg. ðurhwunað 11.2; 3 pl. ðurhwunað 44.2; pret. 3 sg.

ðurhwunode 112.6; 3 pl. ðurh-
wunedon 130.13; pres. p. nsm.
ðurhwunigende 43.3.

ðurhyrnan sv. *currere,* ind.
pret. 3 sg. ðurharn 134.9.

ðus adv. *sic,* 61.10.

ðūsend num. *mille,* gp. ðusenda
52.5.

ðūsendsīðan adv.*millies,* 127.2.

ðū ðe rel. prn. *qui,* ns. ðu ðe
(thirty-seven times); ða ðe 13.9;
np. ge ðe 122.9.

ðwēal sn. *lavacrum,* ap. ðwealu
52.7.

ðwēan sv. *lavare,* pres. p. asm.
ðweandne 104.6.

ðwērnyss sf. *pravum,* ap. ðwer-
nyssa 69.7; cf. ðwyrh.

ðwyrh adj. *pravus,* apf. ðryre
[i.e. ðwyre] 20.6.

ðȳstor, see ðēostor.

U

ufane adv. *sursum,* 37.9.

unācænned adj. (pp.) *ingenitus,*
dsm. unacenedū 45.17.

unāsæcgendlice adv. *ineffabiliter,* unasacgendlice 39.4.

unāstyrod adj. (pp.)*immotus,* nsf.
unastyrod 11.2.

unāwęndendlic adj. *immobilis,*
asf. unawendendlice 19.16;
npm. unawændendlice 130.13.

unbindan sv. *solvere,* imp. pl.
unbindað 122.12.

uncænned adj. (pp.) *ingenitus,*
dsm. uncænedan 120.17.

unclǣne adj. *impurus,* gsf. un-
clænre 72.11.

unclǣnnyss sf. *immunditia,* as.
unclænnysse 28.14.

under prep. *sub,* rv. dat. 75.
14; 85.4; 103.12.

undercrēopan sv. *subripere,* opt.
pres. 3 sg. undercreope 12.14.

underfōn sv. *acceptare, accipere,
admittere, assumere, capere,
excipere, ferre, sumere, suscipere,*
ind. pres. 3 sg. underfehð 141.
11; 142.12; 3 pl. underfoð
136.12; pret. 2 sg. underfenge
39.12; 3 sg. underfeng 53.6;
77.6; 109.8; opt. pres. 3 sg.
underfó 57.8; 1 pl. underfon
68.8; 3 pl. underfon 12.17;
pret. 3 sg. underfenge 54.14;
imp. sg. underfoh 29.8; 68.5;
89.4; 105.18; 124.9; 139.4;
140.4; 147.4; pl. underfoð 119.
16.

undergietan sv.*sentire,* ind. pret.
2 sg. undergæte 103.9; 3 sg.
undergeat 51.2; opt. pres. 1 pl.
undergytan 146.19.

underðeodan wv. *subdere,* inf.
underðeodan 70.12; pres. p.
npm. underðeodende 28.12;
pp. sg. underðeod 91.4; 122.
13; pl. underðeodde 35.4; 59.9.

underwreoðigan wv.*circumfulcire,* pp. nsm. underwreoðod
46.6.

ungelēaffull adj. *incredulus,* nsf.
ungeleaffull 97.7.

ungewæmmed adj. (pp.) *inliba-tus, intactus, inviolatus,* nsf. 50. 15; 54.12; dsn. ungewæmmedū 39.11.

unoferswiðed adj. (pp.) *invictus,* nsf. unoferswiðed 123.17; un-oferswiðod 130.16.

unrōt adj. *tristis,* nsf. unrot 76.1; npm. unrote 85.11.

untrum adj. *infirmus,* apm. un-trume 52.13.

untrumnyss sf. *infirmum,* ap. untrumnysse 62.7; untrūnyssa 44.15; 92.15.

unwæstmbǣre adj. *sterilis,* dsm. unwæstmbærū 132.6.

ūpācuman wv. *provehere,* ind. pres. 3 sg. upalymð [*for* -cymð?] 16.17.

ūpāgān, anv. *oriri,* pp. dsn. upaganū 9.1.

ūpāhębban sv. *efferre, levare, sublevare,* ind. pres. 2 sg. upa-hefst 25.4; opt. pres. 3 sg. np. ahebbe 25.14; imp. sg. upahefe 91.15; 126.4; pp. nsn. upahafene 25.16; asm. upahafenne 70.15.

ūpārǣran wv. *erigere,* opt. pres. 3 sg. uparære 114.1; imp. sg. uparær 125.4; 127.3.

ūpāspringan sv. *oriri,* pp. nsm. upasprungen 27.11; asn. upa-sprunge 25.2.

ūpāstīgan sv. *ascendere,* ind. pret. 3 sg. upastah 45.14.

ūpāwegan sv. *subvehere, vehere,* ind. pret. 3 sg. upawæh 90.1; pp. apn. upawegenan 25.6.

ūplic adj. *supernus,* nsm. upplica 75.12; gsm. upplices 112.8; vsn. uplic 36.1.

upp adv. *sursum,* 91.15.

ūpspring sm. *exortus, ortus,* gs. upspringes 50.1; ds. upspringe 2.10.

ūpspringan sv. *oriri,* pp. npm. upsprungene 136.1.

ūre poss. prn. *noster,* nvs. ure, (fifteen times); gsmn. ures 5.6; 39.10; 44.15; 89.10; 92.15; 104.16; 116.17; gsf. ure 32.8; 33.10; 80.4; 89.14; 110.2; dsn. urum 10.4; dsm. uran 55.4; 105.5; dsf. ure 32.8; 74.15; asm. urne 11.16; 90.1; asfn. ure 68.5; 116.12; 133.12; npf. ure 113.17; gpn. ura 33.11; gpf. ure 120.15; dp. urum (twelve times); ap. ure (twenty-five times).

ūtādrǣfan wv. *pellere,* pp. útadræfde 127.10; dsn. utadræfedū 104.21.

ūtāgān anv. *egredi,* pp. nsm. 34.16; 41.3.

ūtāhębban sv. *levare,* ind. pret. 3 sg. utahóf 66.4.

ūtānȳdan wv. *pellere,* pp. npm. utanydde 36.8; dpf. utanyddum 4.5; 19.15.

ūtfǣreld sn. *egressus,* ns. utfæreld 44.9.

ūtflōwan rv. *manare,* ind. pret. 3 sg. utfleow 78.12.

ūð sf. *praeda,* as. uðe [i. e. huðe] 79.6.

ūtlaga wm. *exul,* ns. utlaga 14.2; np. útlagan 5.13; ap. utlagan 56.2.

uton interj. 3.13; 4.6; 4.7; 6.17; 7.16; 7.17; 7.18; 8.12; 9.2; 16.11; 19.5; 37.12; 45.1; 50.3; 59.4; 61.15; 72.5; 82.4;

87.1; 89.13; 115.16; 115.17; 116.6; 123.11; 129.12.

útrene sm. *excursus*, ns. utrene 44.11.

W

wacigan wv. *vigilare*, opt. pres. 3 sg. wacige 12.18; imp. pl. waciað 19.4; inf. 7.16.

wǽfels smn. *tegimen*, as. wǽfels 103.16.

wǽge wf. *statera*, vs. wǽge 79.5.

wǽl smn. *gurges*, gs. wǽles 52.7; ds. wǽle 25.3; 70.14.

wǽlhréow adj. *crudelis*, *cruentus*, *tyrannus*, nsm. wǽlhreow 52.5; gsm. wǽllhreowes 85.13; asm. wǽllhreowne 83.5; 84.3; wǽlhreowne 139.7.

wǽm, see **wǫm**.

wǽpen sn. *arma*, dp. wǽpnū 61.18; ap. wepna 135.12.

wǽr sf. *foedus*, ap. wǽre 29.2.

wǽsten, see **wésten**.

wǽstm smn. *fructus*, ns. wǽstm 43.20; ds. wǽstme 20.1; 79.9; 104.14.

wǽstmbǽre adj. *fecundus*, *fertilis*, *floridus*, nsf. wǽstmbǽre 20.1; dsmn. wǽstmbǽrū 79.9; apm. wǽstmbǽre (?).

wǽter sn. *aqua*, *lympha*, gs. wǽteres 17.3; 19.15; 49.10; 52.16; as. 48.15; dp. wǽterum 25.2; 25.5; 104.7.

wǽterfǽt sn. *hydria*, np. wǽterfatu 52.16; ap. wǽterfatu 49.10.

wǽtig, see **pǽtig**.

wǽhreft sf. *velum*, ns. wahreft 32.9.

wamb sf. *venter*, ns. 50.11; gs. wambe 75.14; 103.8.

wang sm. *arvum*, dp. wangum 47.5.

wanhál adj. *debilis*, npm. wanhalan 136.12; apm. wanhale 61.7.

wealcan rv. *resolvere*, *volvere*, opt. pres. 3 sg. wealce 121.5; 1 pl. wealcan 24.10.

wealdend sm. *dominator*, *praesul*, nvs. 11.13; 141.1.

weallan rv. *fervere*, opt. pres. 3 sg. wealle 16.7; pres. p. (*fervidus*) npm. weallende 94.4.

wearf, see **ðeorf**.

weaxan rv. *crescere*, *gliscere*, ind. pres. 3 sg. wearð 132.3; 3 pl. weaxað 136.7; opt. pres. 3 pl. weaxan 116.7.

wédan wv. *saevire*, ind. pret. 3 sg. wedde 130.9.

wǫdd sn. *foedus*, ap. wedd 29.2.

weg sm. *via*, as. 6.12; 44.8; vs. 69.1.

wegférend sm. *vians*, dp. wegferendum 6.7.

wegléas adj. *devius*, dsn. wegleasū 24.6.

wel adv. *bene*, 132.15; 133.2.

weler sm. *labium*, gs. weleres 102.3.

wǫll sm. *fons*, ns. wyll 92.7; ds. welle 106.9; vs. 15.10.

welwillende adj. (ptc.) *benignus*, nvsmn. 5.12; 129.1; 141.4; 144.2; asm. welwillendne 49.

11; asn. 116.3; 131.9; vsm. welwillenda 62.2.

welwillendlice adv. *benigne*, 29.8; 138.11.

wensumlice, see wynsumlice.

wēofud smn. *ara*, ns. 79.11; ds. weofode 82.6; as. 143.10.

weorodnyss sf. *dulcedo*, ns. 98.8.

wēpan rv. *flere*, inf. wepan, 56.2; pres. p. npm. wepende 19.6; 22.1; 33.4.

wēpen, see wǣpen.

wer sm. *vir*, as. 50.15.

werhta, see wyrhta.

werlic adj. *virilis*, ns. 38.7; dsn. werlicum 42.2; 43.17.

werlice adv. *viriliter*, 134.10.

werod sn. *acies, agmen, chorus, coetus, exercitus,* nvs. 6.11; 54.5; 117.1; 118.9; 119.17; 137.9; wered 51.7; gs. werodes 115.6; ds. werode 110.12; np. werodu 118.1; dp. werodum 55.11; 57.6; 111.21; 140.6; ap. werodu 47.9; weredu 38.10; vp. werode 119.5.

werod adj. *dulcis*, gsf. werodre 146.17.

werodlice adv. *dulciter*, 7.19.

werst adj. sup. *pessimus*, dsf. wyrstan 29.14; asn. werste 14.8.

wesan, see bēon.

wēsten smn. *desertum, eremus,* gs. westenes 103.12; wæstenes 104.10.

wīdgill adj. *vastus,* gsm. widgilles 104.4.

wīdscrīðol adj. *vagus*, apm. wiðscrīðole 22.14.

wīf sn. *mulier*, dp. wifum, 85.16.

wīglic adj. *bellicus*, apn. wiglice 135.12.

wilddēor sn. *fera, bestia,* gs. wilddeores 28.8; dp. wilddeorum 130.8.

wilfægen adj. *votus, compos,* np. wilfægene 36.15; 84.11; apm. wilfægene 123.6.

willa wm. *voluntas,* ns. 124.2; 130.20.

willan anv. *velle,* ind. pret. 2 sg. woldest 42.20; pres. p. nsm. willende 80.3.

wīn sn. *mustum, vinum,* gs. wines 97.9; ds. wine 94.7; as. win 52.17.

wind sm. *ventus,* np. windas 142.14.

wissigend sm. *rector,* vs. 20.12.

witan swv. *scire,* ind. pres. 2 sg. wast 62.7.

wīte sn. *poena, supplicium,* ds. wite 85.13; gp. witena 139.10; dp. witum 31.10; 130.4; ap. wite 91.19; 127.11; 134.9.

wītega wm. *propheta, vates,* ns. witega 21.2; 72.18; as. witegan 4.8; np. witegan 109.11; gp. witegena 103.20; 118.3; witegana 104.11.

wiðerlēan sn. *compendium,* np. wiðerleane 130.5.

wiðinnan adv. *intrinsecus,* 23.18.

witodlice adv. and conj. *nam, nempe, quidem,* 26.5; 32.9; 47. 5; 62.10; 104.2; 132.3; 132.6; 133.1; 134.5; 142.9.

wiðsacan sv. *negare, renuere, reprobare,* ind. pres. 2 sg. wiðsæcst 68.1; inf. 69.7; pres. p. apm. wiðsacendan 7.2.

wiðstandan sv. *resistere,* opt. pres. 3 sg. wiðstande 72.2.

wiðufan prep. *supra,* w. dat. 137.14.

wiðufen adv. *desuper,* 24.15.

wiðūtan adv. *extra,* wiðutan 62. 14.

wlite sm. *decus,* nvs. 55.4; 65. 16; 69.1; 77.16; 98.4; 105.5; 116.1; 129.1; 137.13; 146.6; ds. 105.10; as. 58.1.

wlitig adj. *decorus,* nvsn. 78. 17; 96.12; nsf. wlitige 19.18; dsn. wlitegum 2.3; 22.10.

wlitigan wv. *decorare,* pres. p. nsm. wlitigende 140.7.

wōdnys sf. *furia,* ap. wodnyssa 132.9.

wǫm smn. *labes, macula,* ds. wæmme 63.3; as. 72.11; 104.9; dp. wommum 47.14.

wōp sm. *fletus,* ds. wope 7.10; 20.5; dp. wopum 13.19; 62.3; ap. wopas 29.8.

wōplic adj. *flebilis,* npmn. woplican 76.3.

word sn. *verbum,* nvs. 36.1; 43.19; gs. wordes 96.14; ds. worde 16.20; 50.16; 85.15; 106. 2; 122.9; 124.12; dp. wordum 94.3.

wōrigan wv. *vagari,* pres. p. (*vagus*) npm. worigende 142. 13; apm. worigende 114.8.

worðian, see wurðian.

woruld sf. *saeculum,* ns. worulde 43.15; gs. worulde 27.16; 33. 16; 35.10; 50.5; 60.12; 69.7; 79.4; 80.14; 104.6; 105.15; 117. 13; 121.7; 122.5; 123.4; 130.3; 133.17; 139.20; weorulde 73. 14; ds. worulde 30.15; 59.11; 74.15; as. worulde 34.11; 105. 11; 139.8; np. worulda 75.7; gp. worulda 49.18; 124.13; 135.2; dp. woruldum 74.9; 117.5; ap. worulda 40.11; 47.2; 55.13; 59.15; 68.12; 83.14; 88.12; 108.16; 112.7; 115.20; 118.20; 120.10; 133.6; 145.7; worulde 1.9; 35.16; 99.11; 106.14; 124. 8; 125.10; 131.4; wurolde 34. 3; woruld 49.18; 135.2.

wrænnyss sf. *petulantia,* ns. wrænnyss 126.12.

wrecan wv. pres. p. (*vindex*) dsm. wrecendum 89.14.

wrixligan wv. *alternare,* pres. p. npm. wrixliende 115.1.

wuldor sn. *gloria, miraculum,* nvs. 1.8; 1.10; 7.15; 8.8; 9. 17; 11.8; 13.11; 16.21; 27.3; 34.1; 35.13; 40.8; 43.12; 44. 21; 46.15; 49.16; 51.11; 52. 19; 54.3; 57.14; 58.11; 59.13; 60.13; 61.9; 72.5; 74.12; 76. 9; 83.11; 84.13; 86.19; 88.11; 88.13; 90.7; 91.22; 106.11; 112.3; 112.16; 118.17; 120.7; 123.7; 123.9; 124.1; 125.8; 130. 19; 131.17; 133.9; 134.17; 138. 16; 139.17; 141.17; 141.18; 142.17; 143.13; 144.2; 145.5; 146.4; gs. wuldres 5.16; 15.8;

F

15.17; 26.12; 113.18; 135.4; ds. wuldre 79.12; 90.2; 135.6; 136.6; 140.7; as. 9.16; 41.2; 59.4; 79.8; 87.8; 89.8; 115.15; 115.17; 115.18; 121.4; 122.3; 133.5.

wuldorbēag sm. *laurea*, dp.wuld-erbeagū 133.1.

wuldorfull adj. *glorificus, 'gloriosus*, dsn. wuldorfullum 108.1; vsf. 111.2; wuldorfulle 75.19; dpf. wuldorfullum 124.16; apn. wuldorfulle 57.12.

wuldrigan wv. *gloriari*, ind. pres. 3 sg. wuldrað 68.11.

wund sf. *vulnus*, gp. wunda 26. 7; 33.13; ap. wunda 20.3; 140. 16; wunde 86.11; wundan 33. 20; 128.6.

wundor sn. *miraculum, mirum*, np. wundra 136.7; gp. wundra 74.5; dp. wundrum 52.11; ap. wundra 102.2.

wundorlic adj. *mirabilis*, asf. wunderlic 42.12; apm. wundorlice 60.10.

wundorlice adv. *mire*, 70.3; wunderlice 69.6.

wundrigan wv. *admirari, mirari, obstupescere,·* ind. pres. 3 sg. wundrað 43.15; 1 pl. wundriað 42.10; 3 pl. wundriað 42.14; 75.7; pres. p. dpm. wundriend-um (?).

wunigan wv. *adesse, constare, exstare, manere*, ind. pres. 3 sg. wunað 37.6; 54.7; 106.13; 115. 20; pret. 3 sg. wunoð 111.6; opt. pres. 3 sg. wunige 26.13; 114.3; imp. sg. wuna 53.13; inf. wunigen 54.11; pres. p. sg. wunigende 27.15; 91.10; 103.

9; 121.6; 145.5; npm. wunigende 55.12.

wurð sn. *pretium*, as. 32.8; 79. 4; 125.2.

wurðe adj. *dignus*, nsm. 47.7.

wurðfull adj. *dignus*, dsm. wurðfullum 79.1; 145.2; vsfn. 82. 17; 144.2.

wurðfullice adv. *digne*, 65.10; 72.10.

wurðigan wv. *colere*, ind. pres. 1 pl. wurðiað 106.15; 120.12; 3 pl. wurðiað 74.17; ger. to wurðigenne 65.10; 141.7; to worðigenne 146.8; pres. p. apm. wurðigende 111.16.

wurðment sfmn. *honor*, ns. 46. 15; 47.16; 49.16; 55.5; 105. 6; 118.17; 125.8; 146.6; wurðmynt 77.18; 112.12; wyrðmynt 35.13; 47.1; 106.12; ds. wurðmente 47.8; 108.5; 137.9; 141. 5; 143.3; wurðmynte 111.19.

wyll, see **well**.

wynsum adj. *suavis*, nsm. 55. 10.

wynsumlice adv. *jocunde*, comp. wensumlicor 98.12.

wyrhta wm. *artifex, factor, opifex*, nvs. 29.4; 75.12; werhta 139.1.

wyrst, see **werst**.

wyrtbræð sm. *aroma, odor*, ns. wyrtbræð 79.7; gp. wyrtbræða 98.9.

Y

ȳdelnyss, see īdelnyss.

yfel sn. *malum*, gs. yfeles 133. 13; ds. efele 136.15; as. 21.

5; dp. yfelum 20.8; 36.13; ap. yfelu 77.1; 119.8; yfele 84. 10.

yfel, adj., see werst.

yfenlytta, see efenhlytta.

ylce, see ilce.

ylding sf. *mora*, ap. yldinge 20. 18.

yldo sbf. *aetas, aevum*, gs. ylde 74.3; 74.4; as. ylde 137.12; 141.20.

ymbryne sm. *circulus*, as. 39.14;

dp. ymbrenū 48.13; emhrynū 27.1.

yrmðsf. *miseria*, ap. yrmða 129.2.

yrnan sv. *currere, cursitare, manare*, ind. pres. 3 pl. yrnað 140. 11; pret. 3 sg. arn 78.12; opt. pres. 3 sg. yrne 44.8; pres. p. nsm. yrnende 39.14.

ẏtemest adj. sup. *ultimus*, nsm. ytemesta 30.9.

ẏð sf. *unda*, ns. yð 17.7; 25.10; 52.18; 78.12.

A

a : fram.

ab : fram.

abditum : dīgolnyss.

abditus : dīgol.

abesse : āweggewītan.

abhorrere : āðracigan.

abjicere : āweorpan.

abluere : āfeormigan.

abscedere : āweggewītan.

absistere : āweggewītan.

absolvere : tōlȳsan.

abstergere : ādrīgan.

abstinentia : fohræfednyss.

abstinere : forhabban.

abstrusus : dīgol.

accendere : onǣlan, ontendan.

acceptabilis : andfænge.

acceptare : underfōn.

accingere : befōn, begērdan.

accipere : underfōn.

accola : inlenda.

acies : trep, werod.

acriter : teartlice.

actus : dǣd.

ad : æt, oð, tō.

adaugere : tōgeīcan.

adesse : ætbēon, wunigan.

adjuturus : tōweard.

adhaerere : tōgeðēodan.

adhibere : gearcigan.

adire : genēosigan.

aditus : infæreld, ingang.

adjutorium : fultum.

adjuvare : gefultumigan, helpan.

admirabilis : tōwundorlic.

admirari : wundrigan.

admittere : underfōn.

adorare : biddan, gebiddan, geēadmēdan.

adornare : gefrætwigan.

adurere : forbærnan.

advenire : tōbecuman.

adventus : tōcyme.

adversus : ongēan.

aeger : ādlig, sēoc.

aegrotus : ādlig.

Aegyptus : Egyptaland.

aequalis : gelīc.

aequor : brym.

aer : lyft.

aetas : yldo.

aeternus : ēce.

aether : rodor.

aethereus : rodorlic.

aevum : ēcnyss, yldo.

affari : sprecan.

affatim : genihtsumlice.

afferre : bringan.

afflare : geondblāwan.

affluus : genihtsum.

agere : dōn.

agmen : werod.

agnoscere : oncnāwan.

agnus : lamb.

alacris : glæd.

alacriter : glædlice.

albescere : hwītigan.

albus : hwīt.

ales : fugel.

alius : ōðer.

alleluia : Godes lof.

allevare : gelīðewǣcan.

alloqui : sprecan.

almus : bālig.

alter : ōðer.

alternare : wrixligan.

altissimum : hēahnyss.

altissimus : hēah.

altor : fōstorfæder.
altum : dēopnyss, hēahnyss.
altus : dēop, hēah, hēalic.
alumnus : fōstercild.
alvus : rif [*for* hrif].
amabilis : luflic.
ambire : gewilnigan.
ambo : bēgen.
amen: swā hit gewurðe, sȳ hit swā.
amicus : frēond.
amor : lufu.
amputare : ofāceorfan.
angelicus : ængelic.
angelus : ængel.
Angli : ænglisc.
Anglicus : ænglisc.
anima : sāwul.
animus : mōd.
annotare : āmearcigan.
annuere : getīðigan, tīðigan.
annus : gēar.
annuus : gēarlic.
ante : ǣr.
antiquus : eald.
antrum : scræf.
anxius : ancsum.
aperire : geopenigan.
apostolus : apostol.
appetere : genēosigan.
apponere : geēcan.
approximare : genēolǣcan.
apte : gelimplice.
aptus : gelimplic.
aqua : wæter.
ara : wēofud.
arbor : trēow.
arca : earc.
arcere : āflȳgan.
archangelus : hēahengel.
ardere : byrnan.
ardor : bryne, fyrwit.
arduum : hēahnyss.
arduus : sticol.
arguere : cīdan.
arma : wǣpen.

armare : gewǣpnigan.
aroma : wyrtbrǣð.
arripere : gegrīpan.
artare : genyrwigan.
artifex : cræftiga, wyrhta.
artium : nearonyss.
artus : lið.
arvum : wang.
arx : hēahnyss.
ascendere : āstīgan, ūpāstīgan.
asper : clincig, teart.
aspicere : besēon.
asserere : secgan.
assistere: ætstandan, ætwunigan.
assumere ꞓ geniman, niman, underfōn.
astare : ætwunigan.
astringere : gewrīðan.
astrum : tungel.
ater : sweart.
atque : and.
atrium : cafertūn.
attendere : begēman.
atterere : tōbrytan.
attingere : æthrīnan, gehrepigan.
attrahere : tēon.
auctor : ealdor.
audere : ðrīstlǣcan.
audire : gehȳran.
auferre : ætbrēdan, āfyrsigan.
augere : geēcan.
aula : heall.
aureus : ænlic.
auris : ēare.
aurora : dægrima, eorendel.
aut : oððe.
auxilium : fultum.
ave : hāl sȳ ðū.
Avernus : hell.
azyma : ðeorf.

B

bajulare : geberan.
balsamum : swētnyss.
baptisma : fulluht.

baptista : fulluhtere.
barathrum : cwicsūsl, hell.
barbarus : hǣðen.
beatus : ēadig.
bellicus : wīglic.
bellum : gewinn.
bene : wel.
benedicere : gebletsigan.
benigne : welwillendlice.
benignus : welwillende.
bestia : wilddēor.
bibere : drincan.
bidens : scēp.
bini : getwinne, twifeald.
blandimentum : geswǣsnyss.
blandus : geswǣs.
bonitas : gōdnyss.
bonus : gōd.
brachium : earm.
bravium : sigelēan.

C

cacumen : hēahnyss.
cadaver : līc.
cadere : feallan.
caducus : gewītendlic.
caecitas : blindnyss.
caecus : blind.
caedere : geslēan.
caedes : slæge.
caelebs : heofonbigende, heofon-lic.
caelestis : heofonlic.
caelicus : heofonlic.
caeligenus : heofoncenned.
caelitus : heofonlice.
caelum : heofon, heofone.
calcare : fortredan.
caligo : dimnyss.
callidus : pætig.
calor : hǣte.
camelus : olfend.
candidus : scīnende.
candor : beorhtnyss.

canere : crāwan, giddigan, herigan, hlēoðrigan, singan.
canor : drēam.
canorus : gedrȳme.
cantare : singan.
canticum : lofsang, sang.
cantus : sang.
capere : befōn, onginnan, underfōn.
captivare : gehæftan.
captivus : hæftling.
caput : hēafod.
cardo : anginn.
carere : ðoligan.
caritas : lufu, sōðlufu.
carmen : lēoð.
carneus : flǣsclic.
caro : flǣsc, līchoma.
carpere : tōteran.
carus : lēof.
castitas : clǣnnyss.
castra : fyrdwīc.
castus : clǣne.
casus : gelimp, mislimp.
catena : racenteg(e).
caterva : hēap.
cedere : ābūgan, geswīcan.
celeber : brȳme.
celebrare : brēman.
celsus : hēah, hēalic.
cena : ǣfengereordung.
censere : dēman.
centeni : hundfeald.
centrum : trendel.
cernere : behealdan, gesēon.
cernuus : ēadmōd, forðāloten.
certe : gewisslice.
certus : cūð, gewiss.
ceterus : ōðer.
chaos : ðrosm.
charisma : gyfu.
chirographum : handgewrit.
chorus : werod.
chrisma : crisma.
christicola : crīsten.

Christus: Crīst.
cibus: męte.
ciere: cīon.
cingere: befōn.
circulus: ymbrene.
circumfulcire: underwreoðigan.
cives: burhlēode.
civis: cæstergewara.
clamare: cleopian.
clarere: scīnan.
claritas: beorhtnyss.
clarus: beorht.
claudere: beclȳsan, belūcan.
clausa: clȳsing.
claustrum: clūse, clȳsing.
clausula: clȳsing.
claviger: cǣgbora.
clavus: nægl.
clemens: mildheort.
clementer: mildheortlice.
clementia: mildheortnyss.
clipeus: scyld.
coaltissimus: hēah.
coetus: werod.
cogere: nēadigan.
cogitare: geðæncan.
cognitus: cūð.
cognomen: nama.
cognoscere: gegaderigan.
colaphus: spurplætt.
colere: gewurðigan, wurðigan.
collegium: gefȳrrǣden.
colligere: gaderigan, gegaderigan.
collis: stīg.
collocare: gelōgigan.
collum: swūra.
color: blēoh.
comes: gesīða.
commodum: behēfnyss.
compago: gefēgednyss.
compar: gemaca.
compassio: besārgung.
compedire: fōtcopsigan.
compendium: wiðerlēan.
comperennis: efenēce.

complere: gefellan.
compos: wilfægen.
comprimere: ofsęttan, ofðriccan.
concedere: forgyfan.
concentus: sang.
concidere: feallan.
concinere: hlēoðrigan, samod-hlēoðrigan.
concio: gegaderung.
concipere: geēacnigan.
concite: hrædlice.
concivis: cæstergewara.
concremare: forswǣlan.
concrepare: hlēoðrigan, swēgan, ðrēagan.
conculcare: fortredan.
condere: behȳdan, gescyppan.
conditor: scyppend.
condolere: besārigan.
conferre: forgyfan, tōbringan, ðurhtēon.
confessio: andetnyss.
confessor: andettære.
configere: āfęstnigan.
confiteri: andettan.
confringere: tōbrecan.
confugere: samodbecuman.
confundere: gedrǣfan.
confusum: gemęngednyss.
congaudere: samodblissigan.
congruus: gedafenlic, ðæslic.
conjungere: geðēodan.
conlaetari: samodblissigan.
conlaudabilis: samodgehęrigend-lic.
conlaudare: samodhęrigan.
conlidere: forceorfan.
conscendere: āstīgan.
conscientia: ingehȳd.
conscius: gewittig.
consecrare: gehālgigan.
consentire: geðafigan.
conserere: gesęttan.
conservare: gehealdan.
consonus: samodgęddung.

consors : efenhlytta.
consortium : gefȳrrǽden.
conspectus : gesihð.
conspicere : bescēawigan.
constare : wunigan.
constituere : gesęttan.
consurgere : ārīsan, samodārīsan.
contactus : hrępung.
contagium : besmitennyss.
contegere : oferhęligan, ðurhtēon.
conterere : forðrǽstan, tōbrytan.
continere : healdan.
contra : ongēan.
contubernium : gemǽnnyss.
cor : heorte.
coram : ætforan.
corona : cynehelm.
coronare : gewuldorbēagigan.
corporeus : līchamlic.
corpus : līchǫma.
corrigere : gerihtlǣcan, ðrēagan.
corruere : hrēosan.
corruptio : gewæmmednyss.
cortex : rind.
coruscare : seīnan.
cosmus : middaneard.
crapula : oferfell.
creare : geedcęnnan, gescyppan.
creator : scyppend.
creatura : gescæft.
crebro : gelōmlice.
credere : gelēfan.
cremare : forswǣlan.
crementum : geēacnung.
crepusculum : ǣfenglōmung.
crescere : weaxan.
crimen : leahtor.
cruciare : cwilmigan.
crudelis : wælhrēow.
cruentus : wælhrēow.
crux : rōd.
cubile : będd.
culmen : hēahnyss.
culpa : gylt.
culpare : leahtrigan.

cultor : bigęnc.
cum : mīd.
cum : ðænne, ðā ðā, ðā ðe.
cumulare : gemǣnigfyldan.
cunabula : cildcradel.
cunctipotens : ælmihtig.
cunctus : eall.
cuneus : hēap.
curare : hǣlan.
currere : āyrnan, ðurhyrnan, yrnan.
currus : cræt.
cursitare : yrnan.
cursus : onryne, ryne.
curvare : gebīgan.
custodia : hyrdrǣden.
custodire : gehealdan, healdan.
custos : hyrde.

D

daemon : dēoful.
damnare : fordēman.
dare : forgyfan, gesęllan, sęllan.
datrix : forgifestre.
Davidicus : Dauidlic.
de : be, of.
debere : sculan.
debilis : wanhāl.
debitor : borhgelda.
debitum : gylt.
debitus : nēadwīs.
decere : gedafenigan.
decidere : feallan.
decipere : beswīcan.
declivus : āurnen.
decorare : gewlitigan, gewuldor-bēagigan, wlitigan.
decorus : wlitig.
decurrere : āyrnan.
decus : wlite.
dedicare : gehālgigan.
defendere : bewęrigan.
defensor : bewęrigend.
deferre : bringan.

deflere : bewēpan.
degere : drohtnigan.
dein : siððan.
deïtas : godcundnyss.
delere : ādīlegian.
delictum : gylt.
delinquere : āgyltan.
demergere : besæncan.
demum : æt nēxtan.
deni : tēonfeald.
dens : tōð, tux.
depellere : ādrǣfan.
deperire : lōsian.
deposcere : biddan.
deprecari : biddan, gebiddan, halsigan.
deprimere : ofðriccan.
depromere : geyppan.
deputare : bescūfan, tęllan.
descendere : niðerāstīgan.
deserere : forlǣtan.
desertum : wēsten.
deservire : ðēowigan.
deses : āsolcen.
desiderare : gewilnigan.
desiderium : gewilnung.
despicere : forsēon.
desuper : wiðufen.
detegere : oferhęligan.
determinare : geęndigan.
Deus : God.
devastare : āwēstan.
devincere : oferswīðan.
devius : weglēas.
devotio : ēstfulnyss.
devotus : ēstfull, ēstfullic.
dexter : swīðre.
diabolus : dēoful. See also *zabulus*.
dicare : gehālgigan.
dicere : gesęcgan, sęcgan.
dicator : gehālgigend.
dictum : cwide.
dies : dæg.
digitus : finger.

dignari : gemedemigan.
digne : wurðfullice.
dignus : wurðe, wurðfull.
diligere : lufigan.
diluculum : ærnemęrgen.
dimergere : see *demergere*.
dimittere : forgyfan.
diremptio : tōdāl.
dirigere : gerihtlǣcan.
diruere : tōweorpan.
dirus : heard, rēðe.
discedere : āweggewītan.
discere : leornigan.
discipulus : leorningcniht.
discutere : tōsceacan.
dissicere : tōsceacan.
dissipare : tōstęncan.
dissolvere : tōlȳsan.
ditare : gewelgian.
diu : lange.
diurnus : dægðerlic.
diversus : mistlic.
dividere : tōdǣlan.
divinitas : godcundnyss.
docere : lǣran.
doctor : lārēow.
doctrina : lār.
documentum : gebisnung.
dogma : lār.
dolere : besārigan.
dolor : sār.
dolus : fācen.
domare : geweldan.
domina : hlǣfdige.
dominator : wealdend.
Dominus : drihten.
domus : hūs.
donare : forgyfan, sęllan.
donec : oððæt.
donum : sęlene.
dormire : slāpan.
drama : hęrung.
dubius : twīniende.
ducere : ādrēogan, gelǣdan, getēon.

ductor : lāttēow.
dudum : gefyrn.
dulcedo : weorodnyss.
dulcis : merig, werod.
dulciter : werodlice.
dum : ðā, ðænne, ðā hwile, ðā ðe.
duodeni : twelfta.
duplex : twifeald.
duplicare : getwifeldan.
durus : heard.
dux : heretoga, lāttēow.

E

ebrietas : druncennyss.
ecce : efne.
ecclesia : gelaðung.
edere : etan.
edere : ācænnan, forðātēon, geyppan.
efferre : ūpāhebban.
efficere : geweorðan.
effluere : becuman, flōwan.
effulgere : scīnan.
effundere : āgēotan.
ego : ic.
egredi : ongēancyrran, ūtāgān.
egregius : æðele.
egressus : ūtfæreld.
elidere : forscræncan.
eligere : gecēosan.
eminus : feorran.
emundare : geclænsigan.
eniti : ācænnan.
ensis : swurd.
eous : ēasterne.
eremus : wēsten.
ergo : eornostlice.
erigere : ūpārǣran.
eripere : generigan.
erratum : gedweld.
error : gedweld.
eruere : generigan.
esse : bēon ; see *non erat*.
esurire : hingrigan.

et : and, ēac swilce.
evacuare : āīdligan, geīdligan.
evertere : āwændan.
ex : be, of.
exaudire : gehȳran.
excelsus : hēalic.
excessus : forgǣgednyss.
excipere : underfōn.
excitare : āstyrigan, āweccan.
excitator : ārǣrend.
excubare : hlynigan.
excursus : ūtryne.
exemplum : bisen.
exercitus : werod.
exhibere : gearcigan.
eximius : hēalic.
exire : gewītan.
exorare : biddan, gebiddan.
exordium : anginn.
exortus : ūpspring.
expandere : āstreccan.
expectare : anbīdigan.
expellere : ādrǣfan.
expiare : āfeormigan.
exposcere : biddan.
exsequi : begietan.
exsolvere : tōlȳsan.
exstare : ðunigan, wunigan (ðunigan ?).
exsurgere : ārīsan.
extendere : āstreccan.
extinguere : ādwǣscan.
extra : wiðūtan.
ex tunc : heononforð.
exuere : bedǣlan.
exul : ūtlaga.
exultare : blissigan.

F

fabrica : getimbrung.
facere : dōn, geweorðan.
facies : ansīen.
factor : wyrhta.
factum : dǣd.

factura : gescæft.
faex : myx.
fallere : lēogan.
falsum : lēasung.
falsus : lēasung.
famen : sprǣc.
famulus : ðēn, ðēowa.
fari : sprecan.
fastidium : āðrētnyss.
fateri : andettan.
fatiscere : ātēorigan.
favere : gefultumigan.
favor : hęrung.
fecundus : ēcen, wæstmbǣre.
feliciter : gesǣliglice.
felix : gesǣlig, sǣlig.
femina : fǣmne.
fenestra : ēahðerl.
fera : wilddēor.
ferocia : rēðnyss.
ferox : rēðe.
ferre : beran, bringan, forberan, gesęcgan, underfōn.
ferreus : īsen.
fertilis : wæstmbǣre.
fervere : weallan.
fervidus : weallende.
fessus : gewǣht.
festivitas : frēolstīd.
festivus : frēols, frēolstīd.
festum : frēols.
festus : frēols.
fibra : æddre.
fidelis : gelēaffull, gelēaflic.
fides : gelēafa.
fidus : getrīwe.
figura : hīw.
filius : bearn, sunu.
finis : ænde, gemǣre.
firmare : getrymman.
firmus : fæst, trum.
flagitare : biddan.
flagrare : byrnan.
flagrum : swingel.
flamen : blǣd, gāst.

flamma : līg.
flammescere : blādesigan, byrnan.
flammeus : līgen.
flatus : blǣd.
flebilis : wōplic.
flectere : gebīgan.
flere : wēpan.
fletus : tēar, wōp.
florere : blōwan.
florescere : scīnan.
floridus : wæstmbǣre.
flos : blōsm.
fluens : flōd.
fluidus : flōwende.
flumen : ēa, flōd.
foedare : befȳlan.
foedus : fūl.
foedus : wǣr, wędd.
foenum : strēow.
fons : węll.
forma : hīw.
formare : gehīwigan, scyppan.
fortis : strang, stranglic.
fortiter : stranglice.
fovere : gehlēowan, gemundigan.
fragilis : tydderlic.
frangere : tōbrecan.
frater : brōðor.
fraus : fācen.
frequenter : oftrædlice.
fretum : brym.
frons : forhēafod.
fructus : wæstm.
frui : brūcan.
fucus : dēg.
fugare : āflȳgan.
fugere : flēon, forflēon.
fulgere : scīnan.
fulgidus : scīnende.
fulvus : geolu.
fundere : āgēotan, āsęndan, geond-gēotan, geondsęndan, sęndan.
funus : hrēaw.
furia : wōdnyss.
futurus : tōweard.

G

Galilea : Galilēaland.
gallus : cocc, hana.
gastrimargia : gīfernyss.
gaudere : blissigan, fægnigan, geblissigan.
gaudium : bliss, gefēa.
gemere : gēomrigan.
geminus : getwinne, twifeald.
gemitus : gēomrung.
generare : ācǣnnan.
genitrix : cynnestre.
genitus : sunu.
gens : ðēod.
gentilis : hǣðen.
genu : cnēow.
genus : cynu.
gerens : ādrēogenlic.
gerere : dōn, geberan.
germanus : brōðor.
germen : sprytting.
gestare : beran.
gestire : gewilnigan, hoppetan.
gestum : dǣd.
gigas : ormǣte.
gignere : ācǣnnan.
gladius : swurd.
gliscere : weaxan.
gloria : wuldor.
gloriari : wuldrigan.
glorificus : wuldorfull.
gloriosus : æðele, wuldorfull.
Graecus : Grēcisc.
grandis : micel.
grates : ðancas.
gratia : forgyfu, gyfu, intinga,
ðanc.
gratis : tōgyfes.
gratuitus : gecwēme.
gratus : gecwēme.
gravare : gehęfegan.
grave : hęfelice.
gravis : hęfig, swār.
graviter : hęfelice.

gremium : bōsm.
gressus : færeld, gang.
grex : ēowde.
gubernare : begēman.
gurges : wǣl.
gustare : onbyrgan.
guttur : ðrote.

H

habere : habban ; see *non habere*.
haerere : geðēodan.
haurire : hladan.
haustus : dręnc, hladung.
hesternus : georstenlic.
hic : hē, sē, ðēs·
hic : hēr, hērðurh.
hinc : heonon ; see *post hinc*.
hirtus : rūh.
hodie : tōdæg.
homo : mann, manna.
honestus : ārwurðe.
honor : wurðment.
hora : tīd.
horrendus : ęgeslic.
horrere : āðracigan.
horridus : lāðlic.
horror : ōga.
hostia : onsǣgednyss.
hostis : fēond.
huc : hidor.
humanitus : męnnisclice.
humanus : męnnisc.
humilis : ēadmōd.
humus : molde.
hydria : wǣterfæt.
hymnifer : lofbǣre.
hymnus : lofsang.

I

idem : ilca.
igneus : fȳren.
ignis : fȳr.
ignoscere : gemiltsigan.
illabi : onāsēon, onāslīdan.

ille : hē, sē.
illigare : gewrīðan.
illinere : begleddigan.
illuc : ðider.
imago : anlīcnyss.
imbuere : tȳn.
immensus : ēce, micel, ormǣte.
immobilis : unāwęndendlice.
immolare : geoffrigan.
immotus : unāstyrod.
immunditia : unclǣnnyss.
imperium : anweald, cynedōm.
impetrare : biddan.
impetus : onrǣs.
impius : ārlēas.
implere : gefellan.
imprimere : ofðriccan.
impurus : unclǣne.
imum : niwolnyss.
in : on, oð.
inclitus : æðele.
incredulus : ungelēaffull.
increpare : ðrēagan.
inde : ðanon.
index : scētefinger.
induere : embscrȳdan.
indulgentia : forgyfenyss, miltsung.
indulgere : gemiltsigan.
ineffabiliter : unāsǣcgendlice.
inferi : hęll, hęllware.
infernus : hęll, hęllic.
inferre : inbringan.
infirmum : untrumnyss.
infirmus : untrum.
informare : gehīwigan.
infundere : āsęndan, onāgēotan,
onāsęndan, onsęndan.
ingenitus : unācænned, uncænned.
ingens : ormǣte.
ingerere : ongebringan.
ingredi : ingān.
inhorrere : anðrācigan.
inimicus : fēond, fēondlic.
initium : anginn.

inlecebra : forspęnning.
inlibatus : ungewæmmed.
inlucere : onlēohtan.
inluminare : onlēohtan.
inlustrare : onlēohtan.
inquam : cweðan.
inquinare : besmītan.
insanus : gewitlēas.
insidia : sęrwung.
insidiare : sęrwian.
insonare : onswēgan.
instare : onwunigan.
instruere : tēon, tȳn.
insuper : ðærtōēcan.
intactus : ungewæmmed.
intendere : begēman.
intentus : geornfull.
inter : betwux.
intercedere : ðingigan.
intercessio : ðingrǣden.
interitus : forwyrd.
intermittere : forlǣtan.
interpellare : ðingigan.
interpolare : betwuxsęndan.
interserere : betwuxsęttan.
interventus : ðingrǣden.
intimum : incundnyss.
intimus : incunde, inlic.
intonare : swēgan.
intrare : infaran, infēran, intōgān.
intrinsecus : wiðinnan.
invenire : gemētan.
investigator : āspyrigend.
invictus : unoferswīðed.
invidus : æfestig, nīðfull.
inviolatus : ungewæmmed.
invocare : cīon.
invocatio : clypung.
ipse : hē, self.
ira : grama.
ire : fēran.
irrogare : onbelǣdan.
irruere : onhrēosan.
is : hē.
iste : ðēs.

item : eft.
iter : sīðfæt.

J

jacentia : īdelgelp.
jacere : licgan.
jactantia : īdelgelp.
jam : eallunga, nū.
janitor : geatweard.
janua : geat.
jecur : lifer.
jejunare : fæstan.
jejunium : fæsten.
Jesus : hǣlend.
jocunde : wynsumlice.
jubar : lēoma.
jubere : bebēodan, gehātan, hātan.
jubilare : fægnigan.
jubilatio : fægnung.
Juda : Jūda.
Judaeus : Jūdēisc.
judex : dēma.
jugis : geornfull, singal.
jugiter : ealneweg.
jugum : geoc.
junctus : geðēodnyss.
jungere : geðēodan.
jussum : hǣs.
justitia : rihtwīsnyss.
justus : rihtwīs.
juvare : gefultumigan.
juvenilis : cildlic.

L

labarum : gūðfana.
labascere : āslīdan.
labes : wǫm.
labi : ætslīdan, āslīdan.
labium : weler.
labor : geswinc.
lac : meolc.
lacerare : slītan, tōteran.
lacrima : tēar.
lactare : sūcan.
laedere : derigan, gederigan.

laetus : blīðe.
lampas : lēohtfæt.
lancea : spere.
languens : ādlig.
languidus : ādlig, sēoc.
languor : ādl.
lapis : stān.
lapsus : senn, slide.
largiri : forgyfan.
largitor : sellend.
large : cystiglice.
latere : lūtigan.
latex : burne.
Latini : lȳdenwaru.
lator : syllend.
latro : scaða.
latus : sīde.
laudabilis : herigendlic.
laudandus : herigendlic.
laudare : geherigan, herigan.
laurea : wuldorbēag.
laureatus : gewuldorbēagod.
laus : herung, lof.
lavacrum : ðwēal.
lavare : āðwēan, ðwēan.
laxare : forgyfan.
laxus : tōlǣten.
lectulus : bedd.
leo : lēo.
levare : āhebban, ūpāhebban, ūtāhebban.
levis : leoht.
lex : ǣ.
libens : lustbǣre.
libenter : lustlice.
liber : bōc.
liber : frēo.
liberare : ālȳsan.
libido : gālnyss.
ligare : gebindan.
lignum : trēow.
lilium : lilīe.
limes : gemǣre.
lingua : gereord, tunge.
linquere : forlǣtan.

lis : cēast, sacu.
locare : gelōgigan.
locus : stōw.
locusta : gærstapa.
longius : feorran.
longus : langsum.
loquela : sprǣc.
loqui : sprecan.
lubricum : slipornyss.
lubricus : fūl, slipor.
lucere : scīnan.
lucerna : fæt.
lucidus : scīnende.
Lucifer : dægsteorra.
lucrari : gestrēonan.
luctus : hēofung.
lugere : hēofigan.
lumbus : lẹnden.
lumen : ēage, lēoht.
luminare : lēohtfæt.
luna : mōna.
luvio : horh.
lux : lēoht.
luxus : gǣlsa.
lympha : wæter.

M

machina : cræft, searu.
macula : wọm.
maculare : gewẹmman.
madere : druncnigan.
maeror : gnornung.
magister : lāreow.
magnalia : mǣrða.
magnifice : mǣrlice.
magnus : micel.
magus : tungelwītega.
major : māra.
malignus : āwyrged.
malle : swīðorwillan.
malum : yfel.
manare : ūtflōwan, yrnan.
mane : ǣrmẹrgen.
mane : ǣrnemẹrgen.
manere : wunigan.

manus : hand.
mare : sǣ.
martyr : cȳðere, ðrōwǣre.
martyrium : martyrdōm.
mater : mater, mōder.
maxime : swīðost; see *quam maxime*.
maximus : mǣsta.
medela : lǣcedōm.
medicina : lǣcedōm.
medicus : lǣce.
meditari : smēagan.
mel : hunig.
mellifluus : hunigswēte.
melodus : gedrȳme.
melos : lof.
membrum : lim.
meminisse : gemunan.
mendax : lēas.
mens : mōd.
mensis : mōnað.
mercari : gebycgan.
merere, mereri : geearnigan.
mergere : besæncan.
meridies : middæg, midnedæg.
meritum : forgeearnung, geearnung.
micare : scīnan.
miles : cẹmpa.
mille : ðūsend.
millies : ðūsendsīðan.
minister : ðēn.
ministrare : ðēnigan.
mirabilis : wundorlic.
miraculum : wuldor, wun dor.
mirari : wundrigan.
mire : wundorlice.
mirum : wundor.
miscere : gemǣngan.
miser : earming.
miserari : gemiltsigan.
miseria : yrmð.
mitescere : gelīðewǣcan.
mittere : āsẹndan.
mitis : līðe.

mixtum : gemęngednyss.
moderare : gemeagan.
modo : nū.
modulari : drēman.
modulus : drēam.
moles : hęfe.
molestia : hęfigtēmnyss.
molestum : hęfigtēmnyss.
momentum : handhwīl.
monachus : munuc.
mons : dūn.
monstrare : geswuteligan.
monstrum : scīnhīw.
mora : ylding.
morbidus : ādlig.
morbus : ādl.
mordere : slītan.
mors : dēað.
mortalis : dēadlic.
mortuus : dēad.
mos : ðēaw.
motus : sterung.
mucro : swurd.
mulier : wīf.
multum : miclum.
multus : feala, mænig, micel.
mundanus : middaneardlic.
mundare : geclænsigan.
mundus : middaneard, mideard.
mundus : clæne.
munerare : gewelgian.
munimen : embtrymmung.
munus : gyfu, lāc.
murmur : murcnung.
mustum : nīwe wīn.
mutare : āwændan.
mysterium : gerȳne.
mystice : gerȳnelice, rȳnelice.
mysticus : gerȳnelic, gerȳnu, rȳnelic.

N

nam : witodlice.
nasci : ācænnan.
natalis : gebyrdtīd.

natio : mǣgð.
natus : āncænned, bearn, sunu.
nauta : scypman.
naviter : cāflice.
ne : nā, ne.
nec : nā, ne.
nec non : ēac swilce.
nectar : hunigtēar.
nefas : mān.
negare : wiðsacan.
nemo : nænig.
nempe : witodlice.
nequitia : hinderscipe.
nescire : nytan.
nex : cwalu.
nexus : bęnd.
nihil : nāht.
nimbus : scūr.
nimis : swīðe, ðearle.
nisus : hogung.
nitere : scīnan.
nitidus : scīnende.
nitor : beorhtnyss.
niveus : snāhwīt.
nobilis : æðele.
nocens : dęrigendlic.
nocere : dęrigan.
nocte : nihtes.
nocturnus : nihtlic.
nomen : nama.
non : nā, ne.
nona : nōnsang.
non erat, non fuit : næs.
non habere : nabban.
noscere : cunnan, oncnāwan.
noster : ūre.
notus : swutol.
novus : nīwe, nēowiende.
nox : niht.
noxa : dara.
noxius : dęrigendlic.
nubes : genip.
nubilum : genip.
nudatus : nacod.
nullus : nān.

numen : God, miht.
numerus : getæl.
nunc : nū.
nuntiare : cȳðan.
nuntius : bodung, bydel.
nusquam : næfre.
nutus : miht.

O

O : ēalā, ō.
ob : for.
oblectare : gelustfulligan.
obruere : ofhrēosan.
obscurum : forsworcennyss.
obscurus : deorc, forsworcenlic.
obsequi : gehērsumigan.
obserere : bewindan.
observare : healdan.
obstrusus, see *abstrusus*.
obstupescere : wundrigan.
obtemperare : gehērsumigan.
obtentus : ðingrǣden.
occasus : setlgang.
occultus : dīgol.
occurrere : becuman, ongēancuman.
ociter : hrædlice.
oculus : ēage.
odor : wyrtbrǣð.
offendere : ætspurnan.
offensum : ætspyrning.
offerre : geoffrigan, offrigan.
olim : gefyrn.
oliva : elebēam.
Olympus : rodor.
omnipotens : ælmihtig.
omnis : ǣlc, eall.
opifex : wyrhta.
opimus : genihtsum.
ops : spēd.
optare : gewīscan.
optimus : sēlosta.
oraculum : bēn.
orare : biddan, gebiddan.
oratio : bēn.

orbatus : blīnd.
orbis : ymbhwerft.
orbita : hwēollāst.
ordinare : geendeberdigan.
ordo : ændebyrdnyss.
organum : drēam.
origo : ordfruma.
oriri : ūpāgān, ūpāspringan, ūp-springan.
ornare : gefrætwigan.
orphanus : stēopcild.
ortus : ūpspring.
os : bān.
os : mūð.
ostendere : ætȳwan.
ovis : scēp.

P

palam : openlice.
pallere : blācigan.
pallor : blācung.
pandere : geyppan.
pangere : geyppan.
pannus : cildclāð.
par : gelīc.
Paraclitus : frōfer, Frōfergāst.
Paradisus : neorxnewang.
parare : gearcigan.
parcere : ārigan.
parcitas : spearnyss.
parens : fæder, mōder.
parere : ācænnan.
pariter : samod.
pars : dǣl.
parsimonia : forhæfednyss.
partim : dǣlmǣlum.
parturire : ācænnan, cænnan.
partus : bearn, cenning, geēacnung, sunu.
parvulus : cild.
parvus : gehwæde.
pascere : fēdan.
Pascha : Ēastre.
paschalis : ēasterlic.

passio: ðrōwung.
pastor: hyrde.
pastus: fōda.
pater: fæder.
paternus: fæderlic.
pati: ðoligan, ðrōwigan.
patibulum: gealga.
patientia: geðeld.
patrare: gefręmigan.
patria: ēðel.
patriarcha: hēahfæder.
patrocinium: mundbyrd.
pavere: forhtigan.
pavescere: āforhtigan, forhtigan.
pavor: ōga.
pax: sibb.
peccamen: senn.
peccare: sengigan.
peccator: senfull.
peccatum: senn.
pectus: brēost.
pellere: ādræfan, cnyssan, ūtā-dræfan, ūtanȳdan.
pendere: hangigan.
penetrale: innoð.
penetrare: ðurhfaran.
penitus: eallunga.
per: be, geond, ðurh.
per aevum: ēcelice.
peragere: geęndigan, gefręmigan.
peraridus: forscruncen.
percutere: geslēan.
perdere: forlēosan, forspillan.
perducere: gebringan.
perenne: ēcelice.
perennis: ēce, ēcelic.
perenniter: ēcelice.
perferre: ðoligan.
perficere: fullfręmman.
perfidus: gelēaflēas.
perfrui: brūcan.
perfundere: geondgēotan.
pergere: gān.
perimere: losian, ofslēan.
perire: losian.

perlustrare: geondscīnan.
perlustrator: geondlēohtend.
permanere: ðurhwunigan.
perpes: ēce.
perpetim: ēcelice.
perpetuum: ēcnyss.
persolvere: gelæstan.
personaliter: hādelice.
personare: swēgan.
persultare: swēgan.
perurere: forbærnan.
pervenire: becuman.
pervicax: gemāh.
pervigil: ðurhwacol.
pervius: ðurhfere.
pervocare: gelængan.
pes: fōt.
pessimus: werst.
pestis: cwild.
petere: biddan, fēran, gefaran, gefēran, genēosigan.
petra: stān.
petulantia: wrænnyss.
phantasma: gedwimor.
Pharao: dēoful.
piaculum: mān.
piceus: picen.
pie: ārfæstlice.
pietas: ārfæstnyss.
pignus: tudder.
pigritari: sleacgigan.
pinguere: āmȳtan.
piscator: fiscere.
pius: ārfæst.
placatus: glæd.
placidus: glæd.
planare: gesmēðigan.
planta: fōtwelm.
plasma: gescæft.
plasmare: gescyppan.
plasmator: scyppend.
plaudere: fægnigan.
plebs: folc.
plene: fullice.
plenus: full.

pneuma : gāst.
poculum : dręnc, dręncfæt.
poena : wīte.
poenitentia : behrēowsung.
pollere : ðēon.
polluere : besmītan.
polus : heofon, heofone.
pompa : glęnga.
pomus : æppel.
ponere : gelęcgan, sęttan.
pontifex : biscop.
pontus : brym, sǣ.
populus : folc.
porrigere : ārǣcan.
porta : geat, infǣreld.
portare : beran.
poscere : biddan, gebiddan.
posse : magan.
possidere : āhnigan, geāhnigan.
post : æfter, siððan, ðǣræfter.
post hinc : siððan.
postulare : biddan.
potens : mihtig.
potenter : mihtelice.
potentia : miht.
potentialiter : mihtelice.
potestas : anweald, miht.
potiri : brūcan.
potus : dręnc.
praebere : gearcigan.
praeceps : scefe.
praeceptum : gebod.
praecinere : bodigan, hlēoðrigan.
praecipere : bebēodan.
praecipue : hēalice.
praeco : bydel.
praeconium : bēn, bodung.
praeda : rēaflāc, ūð.
praedicare : bodigan.
praedicere : foresęcgan.
praeditus : gewelegod.
praemium : mēd.
praeparare : gearcigan.
praepotens : foremihtig.
praesagus : forewītegende.

praesens : andweard.
praesentare : andweardigan.
praesepe : binn.
praestare : gearcigan, getīðigan, mǣrigan, tīðigan.
praestolari : anbīdigan.
praesul : biscop, wealdend.
praeterire : forðgewītan.
praevius : forestæppende.
pravum : ðwērnyss.
pravus : ðwȳrh.
precari : biddan.
precatus : bēn, forbēn.
pretiosus : dēorwurðe.
pretium : wurð.
prex : bēn.
primas : ealdor.
primordium : anginn, fruma, on-āginn.
primum : ǣrest.
primus : forma, fyrmst.
princeps : ealdor.
principalis : ealdorlic.
principium : anginn.
pro : for.
probare : āfandigan, sprecan.
probrum : mān.
procedere : forðstæppan.
processus : forðstæpping.
procul : feor.
prodere : forðātēon, gebēcnan, geyppan.
prodesse : foregewissigan, fręmigan.
prodigium : forebēcn.
prodire : forðstæppan.
producere : forðātēon.
proelium : gewinn.
proferre : forðbringan.
profluus : genihtsum.
profundere : āgēotan.
profundum : dēopnyss.
profundus : dēop.
proles : bearn, tudder.
promere : geyppan.

promicare: scīnan.
promissum: behāt.
promittere: behātan.
prompte: hrædlice.
promptus: hræd.
pronuntiare: gecȳðan.
pronus: ēadmōd.
prope: gehende.
properare: ofstlice.
propheta: wītega.
propinare: scencan.
propinquus: gehende.
propitiare: gemiltsian.
propitius: milde.
proprius: āgen.
propter · for.
prorsus: eallunga.
prosperum: gesundfulnyss.
prospicere: bescēawigan.
protegere: gescildan.
protinus: ðærrihte, ðærrihtes.
protomartyr: forma cȳðere, forma ðrōwære.
provehere: ūpācuman.
provide: foreglēawlice.
providus: foreglēaw.
proximus: gehende, nēoxta.
prudens: snoter.
psallere: singan.
psalmus: sealmsang.
publicus: swutol.
pudicitia: clænnyss.
pudicus: clæne, sidefull.
pudor: clænnyss.
puella: mæden.
puer: cild.
puerpera: hyseberðor.
puerulus: cild.
pugillus: fēst.
pugnare: fechtan.
pulvis: dūst.
punire: gewītnigan.
purgare: āfeormian.
purpura: godewebb.
purus: clæne.

Q

qua: ðænne.
quadragenarius: fēowertigfeald.
quaerere: sēcan.
quaerimonia: ceorung.
quaesere: begietan. biddan.
quaestus: bēn.
qualitas: gehwilcnyss.
quam: hwu.
quam maxime: ealra **swīðost**.
quantocius: hrædlice.
quartus: fēorða.
quatere: tōcwīsan.
quaterni: fēower.
-*que*: and.
quemadmodum: swā swā.
qui: ic ðe, sē. sē ðe. ðe. ðū ðe.
quia: forðām, forðām ðe. forðan.
quid: tō hwī.
quidam: sum.
quidem: witodlice.
quies: stilnyss.
quietus: gedēfe.
quique: ic ðe. sē ðe.
quire: magan.
quis: hwā, hwilc.
quislibet: swā hwilc.
quisquis: swā hwā, swā hwā swā.
quisquam: ænig.
quisque: gehwilc.
quocunque: swā hwider swā.
quondam: gefyrn.
quoque: ēac swilce.

R

radiare: scīnan.
radicare: āwyrtwalian.
radius: lēoma.
rapere: ætbrēdan. gelæccan. onfōn.
rapina: rēaflāc.
reatus: scyld. senn.

reboare: hlynian.
recedere: āweggewītan.
rector: reccend, wissigend.
rectus: riht.
recursus: ongēancyme, ryne.
reddere: āgyfan, āgyldan, dōn.
redemptio: ālȳsednyss.
Redemptor: Ālȳsend.
redimere: ālȳsan.
redire: gehwerfan, ongēangehwyrfan.
reditus: geancyrr.
redolere: stēman.
reducere: geondhwerfan, ongēanbringan.
refercire: gefellan.
referre: gereccan, ongēanbringan.
reficere: gelīðewǣcan.
reflectere: gebīgan.
reformare: geedstaðeligan.
refrenare: geweldan.
refrigerare: gecēlan.
refulgere: scīnan.
refundere: āgēangesǣndan, āgēotan, geondgēotan, ongēansendan.
regere: gewissigan.
regina: cwēn.
regius: cynelic.
regnare: rīxigan.
regnum: rīce.
regressus: ongēancyme.
regula: regol.
relevare: gelīðewǣcan.
religare: gewrīðan.
relucere: scīnan.
remedium: lǣcedōm.
remissio: forgyfenyss.
remittere: forgyfan, ongēansendan.
removere: āsindrigan.
remunerator: geedlēanend.
renasci: geedcennan.
reniti: healdan.
renuere: wiðsacan.
repellere: ādrǣfan.

rependere: āgyldan.
repente: fǣrlice.
replere: gefellan.
reprimere: ofðriccan.
reprobare: wiðsacan.
reptans: slincend.
reputare: forðæncan.
requies: rest.
requirere: sēcan.
res: gesceaft, ðing.
reserare: geopenigan.
residere: sittan.
resistere: wiðstandan.
resolvere: tōlȳsan, wealcan.
resonare: singan, swēgan.
respicere: behealdan, besēon.
resplendere: scīnan.
respuere: forsēon.
restituere: edstaðoligan.
resultare: swēgan.
resurgere: ārīsan.
resuscitare: āweccan.
retexere: gereccan.
retinere: gehæftan, healdan.
retroagere: onbæcgedōn.
retundere: ætstandan.
reus: scyldig.
revertere: gecyrran, ongēangecyrran.
rex: cyng.
rimari: smēagan.
rite: rihtlice.
rivulus: rīð.
robur: strængð.
robustus: strang.
rogare: biddan.
rogitare: biddan.
roseus: rēad, rōsen.
rota: hweogul.
ruber: rēad.
rubescere: rēadigan.
ructare: balcettan.
ruere: hrēosan.
rumpere: tōbrecan.
rutilare: glitinian.

S

sacer : hālig.
sacerdos : sācerd.
sacramentum : gerȳne.
sacrare : gehālgigan.
sacratus : hālig.
sacrosanctus : hālig.
saeculum : woruld.
saepire : embhęgigan.
saepius : oftrædlice.
saevire : wēdan.
saevus : rēðe.
saltem : hūruðinga.
salubris : hālwęnde.
salus : hæl.
salutare : gegrētan.
salvare : gehǣlan.
salve : hāl sȳ ðū.
salvus : hāl.
sanare : gehǣlan, hǣlan.
sancire : gehālgigan.
sanctitas : hālignyss.
sanctus : hālig.
sanitas : hǣl.
sanguineus : blōdig.
sanguis : blōd.
sapor : swæc.
sarcina : berðen.
satagere : hōgigan.
satiare : geweldan.
Sator : Hǣlend.
saucius : gewǣht.
scandalum : æswicung.
scandere : āstīgan.
scelus : scyld.
sceptrum : cynegyrd.
scindere : tōslītan.
scire : cunnan, witan.
scribere : āwrītan.
scriptum : gewrit.
scrutator : smēagend.
scutum : scyld.
se : hē, self.
secretum : dīgolnyss.

secretus : dīgol.
secundare : gesundfulligan.
secundo : oðer sīðan.
secundus : gesundfullod.
sed : ac.
sedere : sittan.
sedes : setl.
sedulus : geornfull, singal.
segregare : āsindrigan.
semen : sǣd.
semita : sīðfæt.
semper : ǣfre, simle.
sempiternus : ēce.
senatus : rǣdgift.
senex : eald.
sensus : andget, sefa.
sentire : gefrēdan, undergytan.
septemplex : seofonfeald.
septies : seofonsīðan.
septiformis : seofonfeald.
sequi : æfterfyligan, folgigan,
    fyligan.
sera : scettels.
serenus : līðe, smilte.
series : ændebyrdnyss.
sermo : sprǣc.
serpens : næddre.
sertum : cynehelm.
servare : gehealdan.
servilis : ðēowtlic.
servire : ðēowigan.
servulus : ðēowtling.
servus : ðēowa.
sese : hē, self.
sexus : hād.
si : gyf.
sic : swā, ðus.
sicut : swā swā.
sidereus : tunglen.
sidus : tungel.
signare : geinsegeligan, getācni-
    gan.
signifer : tācenbora.
signum : tācen.
silentium : swīge.

similis : gelīc.
simplex : ānfeald.
simul : samod.
sinceritas : sēfernyss.
sine : būtan.
sinere : geðafigan.
singularis : ānfeald.
sistere : bēon.
sobrius : sēferlic, sēfre.
socius : gefēra.
sol : sunne.
solamen : frōfer.
solitus : gewunelic.
solium : cynesetl.
sollemne : simbelnyss.
sollemnis : simbel.
solum : molde.
solus : ān.
solvere : ālȳsan, gelǣstan, tōgelȳsan, tōlȳsan, tōslūpan, unbindan.
somniare : swefnigan.
somnium : swefn.
somnolentia : slāpolnyss.
somnolentus : slāpol.
somnus : slǣp.
sonare : swēgan.
sopor : slǣp.
soporus : slǣp.
sorbere : forswelgan.
sordes : horh.
sordidare : gehorwigan.
sordidus : fūl, borig.
sors : hlot.
spargere : geondstrēdan.
spatium : fæc.
speculator : bescēawære.
spernere : forsēon.
spes : hiht, hopa.
spiculum : lēoma, strǣle.
spiramen : blǣd, gāst.
spirare : ēðigan, orðigan.
spiritalis : gāstlic.
spiritus : gāst.
splendere : scīnan.

splendidus : beorht, scīnende.
splendor : beorhtnyss, bryhtnyss.
sponsa : brēd.
sponsus : brȳdguma.
sputum : spātl.
stadium : furlang.
stare : standan.
statera : wǣge.
statuere : gesęttan.
stella : steorra.
stemma : æðelborenyss.
sterilis : unwæstmbǣre.
stipes : bōg.
stirps : cynren.
stola : gyrla.
strenue : hrǣdlice.
strenuus : stranglic.
strophium : gyrdel.
studium : gecneordnyss.
suavis : wynsum.
suavisonus : swētswēge.
sub : under.
subdere : underðēodan.
subdolus : fācenfull, fācenfullic.
sublevare : ūpāhębban.
sublimis : hēalic.
sublimitas : hēalicnyss.
subripere : undercrēopan.
subruere : hrēosan.
substantia : edwist.
subtrahere : ætbrēdan.
subvehere : ūpāwegan.
subvenire : gehelpan.
successus : æfterfyligendnyss.
sufferre : forðeldegan.
suffragium : help.
suggerere : tihtan.
sumere : niman, underfōn.
summus : hēalic.
super : ofer.
superare : oferswīðan.
superbia : mōdignyss.
superbus : mōdig.
supernus : heofonlic, ūplic.
supplex : ēadmōd, ēadmōdlic.

supplicare : biddan, halsigan.
supplicatio : bēn, halsung.
suppliciter : ēadmōdlice.
supplicium : wīte.
supra : ofer, wiðufan.
surgere : ārīsan.
sursum : ufane, upp.
suscipere : onfōn, underfōn.
suscitare : ārǣran, āwęccan.
suspendere : āhōn.
suspendium : hȳnð.
suus : his, heora (see hē).

T

tacitus : stille.
taedium : āðrētnyss.
taeter : sweart.
talis : swile.
tam : swā.
tandem : æt nēxtan.
tangere : hręppan.
tanto : swā.
tantum : ān.
Tartara, -us : hęll.
tegimen : wǣfels.
tellus : eorðe.
telum : flān.
temperare : gemetegian.
templum : tempel.
templare : onginnan.
tempus : tīd, tima.
tenax : fæsthafol.
tendere : āðęnigan, ęfstan.
tenebrae : ðēostor.
tener : gung.
tenere : healdan, niman.
tenuare : āðinnian.
tepescere : ācōligan.
ter : ðriwa.
terere : tōbrytan.
tergere : ādrīgan.
terminus : geęndung, gemǣre.
terra : eorðe.
terrenus : eorðlic.
terrestris : eorðlic.

terror : ōga.
tertius : ðridda.
testari : gesēðan.
testimonium : gewittnyss.
testis : gewita.
thalamus : brēdbūr.
theologus : drihtwurðe.
thronus : ðrymsetl.
timere : ondrǣdan.
timor : ęge.
tingere : bedyppan.
tollere : ætbrēdan, āhębban, niman.
tonans : ælmihtig.
torpere : āswindan.
torpidus : slāw.
torpor : slǣwð.
torridus : gebrǣden.
tortor : cwellære.
totus : eall.
tradere : bescūfan, betǣcan.
trahere : getēon, tēon, tōgetēon.
trames : sīðfæt.
transferre : gebringan.
transire : gewītan, ðurhfaran.
transitus : oferfæreld.
tremere : beofigan.
tremescere : beofigan.
tribuere : forgyfan.
tribunal : dōmsetl.
tribus : mǣgð.
Trinitas : ðrynnyss.
trinus : ðrēofeald, ðrilic, ðrinen, ðrȳ.
triplex : ðrēofeald.
tristis : unrōt.
triumphalis : sigorlic.
triumphare : sigorigan.
triumphus : sige.
trophaeum : sige.
tu : ðū.
tueri : gescildan.
tumescere : tōðindan.
tumulus : byrgen.
tunc : ðā, ðænne ; see *ex tunc*.
turba : mænigu.

turbidus : drēfende, gedrēfed.
turbo : gedrēfednyss, ðoden.
turma : hēap.
tutare : bewęrian.
tulus : orsorh.
tuus : ðīn.
tyrannus : wælhrēow.

U

ubique : æghwǣr.
ulna : earm.
ultimus : ȳtemest.
ululare : ðoterigan.
umbra : sceadu.
umquam : ǣfre.
una : samod.
unctio : smęrung.
unda : ȳð.
unde : forðī, ðanon.
undique : æghwanone.
ungula : clāwu, hōc.
unicus : āncænned, ānlic.
unigenitus : āncænned.
unitas : ānnyss.
unus : ān.
urbs : burh.
urgere : onsīgan.
usque : oð.
usus : brēce, gewuna.
ut : swā, swā swā, ðæt.
uterque : æghwæðer.

V

vacare : āīdligan.
vagari : wōrian.
vagus : wīdscrīðol, wōrigende.
valde : ðearle.
valere : magan, swīðrigan.
vanitas : īdelnyss.
vanum : īdelnyss.
vapor : hǣte.
vastare : berȳpan.
vastus : wīdgill.
vates : scop, wītega.
ve : ne.

vecordia : gewitlēast.
vegetare : gestrangigan.
vehere : ūpāwegan.
vel : oððe.
velle : willan.
velum : wāhreft.
velut : swā swā.
venenum : āttor.
venerandus : ārwurðe.
venerare : ārwurðigan.
venia : forgyfenyss.
venire : cuman.
venter : innoð, wamb.
venturus : tōweard.
ventus : wīnd.
verax : sōðfæst.
verber : swingel.
verbum : word.
vere : sōðlice.
vergere : onsīgan.
veritas : sōðfæstnyss.
vernaculus : ðēow.
vero : sōðlice.
versari : drohtnigan.
vertere : āwændan.
verus : sōð.
vesanus : gewitlēas.
vesper : ǣfen.
vester : ēower.
vestigium : fōtswæð.
vestire : gefrætwigan.
velare : forbēodan.
vetitus [sic] : eald.
vetus : eald.
vexillum : gūðfana.
via : weg.
vians : wegfērend.
vibrare : ræscan.
vicis : gewrixl.
victima : offrung, onsǣgednyss.
victor : sigefæst, sigriend.
victrix : sigefæst.
videre : gesēon.
vigere : ðēon.
vigilare : wacigan.

vigor : strængð.
vincere : oferswīðan.
vinculum : bẹnd.
vindex : wrẹcende.
vindicare : becēpan.
vinum : wīn.
vir : wer.
virginalis : mǣdenlic.
virgineus : mǣdenlic.
virgo : fǣmne, mǣden.
virilis : werlic.
viriliter : werlice.
viror : grēnnyss.
virtus : mǣgen, miht.
vis : mǣgen.
viscus : innoð.
visere : genēosigan.
visitare : genēosigan.
visus : gesihð.
vita : līf.
vitalis : līflic.
vitare : forbūgan.
vitium : leahtor.

vivere : libban.
vividus : libbende, līflic.
vivus : līflic.
vocare : cīon, gecīgan.
vocitare : gecīgan.
volitare : flēon.
voluntas : willa.
volvere : betyrnan, wealcan.
volum : behāt, bēn, gewilnung.
votus : wilfægen.
vox : stefn.
vulnerare : gewundigan.
vulnus : wund.
vultus : andwlita.

Y

yrcus, see *hirtus*.

Z

zabulus : dēoful, scucca.　See also *diabolus*.

YALE STUDIES IN ENGLISH.

ALBERT S. COOK, EDITOR.

Lightning Source UK Ltd.
Milton Keynes UK
UKHW010803211118
332624UK00007B/187/P